CLASSICAL KIDS

CLASSICAL KIDS

An Activity Guide to Life in Ancient Greece and Rome

LAURIE CARLSON

CHICAGO
REVIEW
PRESS

CIP:Library of Congress Cataloging-in-Publication Data

Carlson, Laurie M., 1952–
Classical kids : an activity guide to life in Ancient Greece and
Rome / Laurie Carlson.
        p.   cm.
Includes bibliographical references.
Summary: Demonstrates life in ancient Greece and Rome, and the
contributions of those cultures to modern civilization, through
hands-on activities such as making a star gazer, chiseling a clay
tablet, and weaving Roman sandals.
ISBN 1-55652-290-8
1. Greece–Social life and customs–Juvenile literature. 2. Rome–
Social life and customs–Juvenile literature. 3. Creative
activities and seat work–Juvenile literature. [1. Greece–
Civilization–To 146 B.C. 2. Rome–Civilization. 3. Handicraft.]
I. Title.
DE71.C26   1998
938-dc21   97-52676
                                                                  CIP
                                                                  AC

Design and illustrations ©1998 by Fran Lee

©1998 by Laurie Carlson
All rights reserved
First edition
Published by Chicago Review Press, Incorporated
814 North Franklin Street
Chicago, Illinois 60610
ISBN 1-55652-290-8
Printed in the United States of America

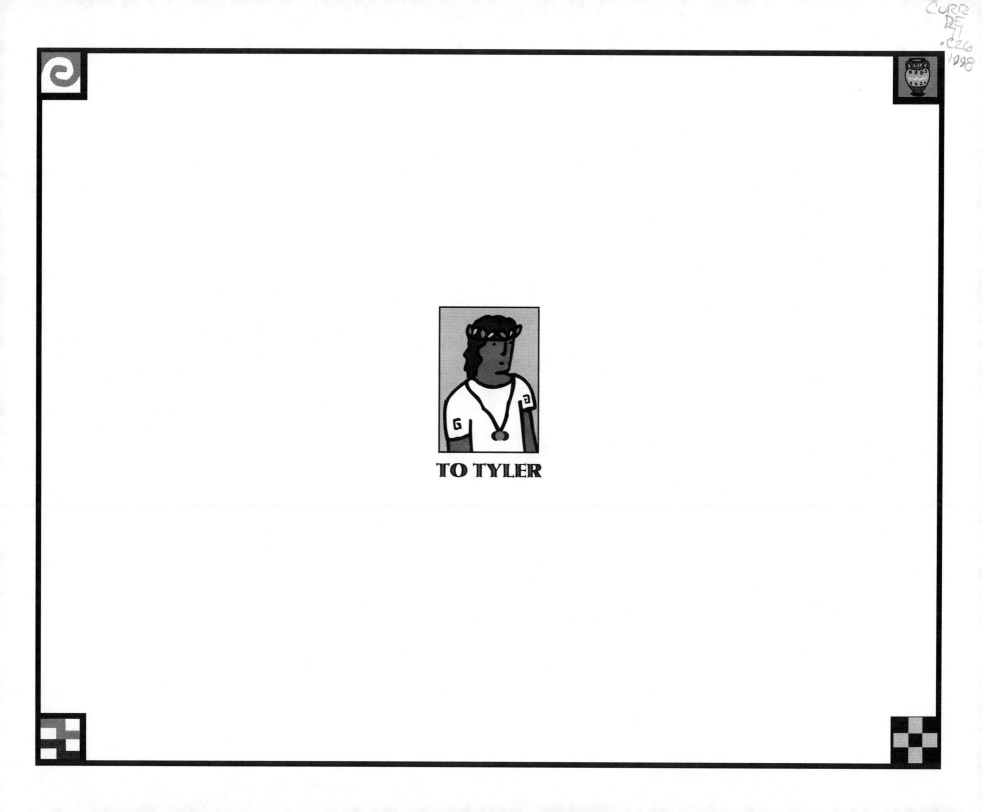

TO TYLER

*Let no one be slow to seek wisdom when
he is young nor weary in the search
when he has grown old.*
—Epicurus, Greek philosopher, 341–270 B.C.

Carpe diem!
Seize the day!

Acknowledgments

Thank you to Cynthia Sherry, Lisa Rosenthal-Hogarth, Rita Baladad, Fran Lee,
Curt and Linda Matthews, Mark Suchomel, Kathy Mirkin, Mark Voigt,
Susan Sewall, and the rest of the team at Chicago Review Press.
A huge thanks for another enjoyable project together!

CONTENTS

TIME LINE

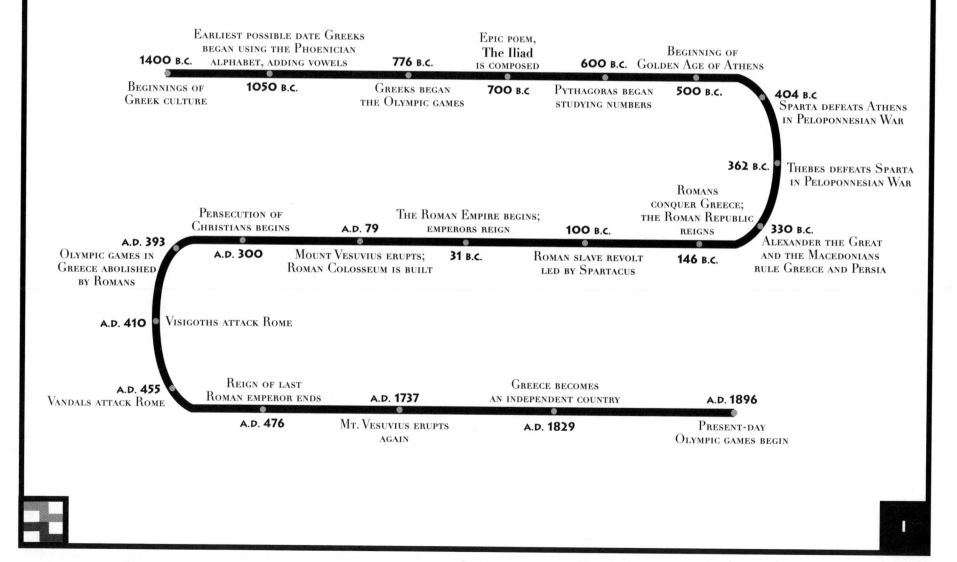

1400 B.C. Earliest possible date Greeks began using the Phoenician alphabet, adding vowels

776 B.C.

Epic poem, **The Iliad** is composed

600 B.C. Beginning of Golden Age of Athens

Beginnings of Greek culture

1050 B.C.

Greeks began the Olympic games

700 B.C.

Pythagoras began studying numbers

500 B.C.

404 B.C Sparta defeats Athens in Peloponnesian War

362 B.C. Thebes defeats Sparta in Peloponnesian War

Romans conquer Greece; the Roman Republic reigns

330 B.C. Alexander the Great and the Macedonians rule Greece and Persia

Persecution of Christians begins

A.D. 79

The Roman Empire begins; emperors reign

100 B.C.

A.D. 393

Olympic games in Greece abolished by Romans

A.D. 300

Mount Vesuvius erupts; Roman Colosseum is built

31 B.C.

Roman slave revolt led by Spartacus

146 B.C.

A.D. 410 Visigoths attack Rome

A.D. 455 Vandals attack Rome

Reign of last Roman emperor ends

A.D. 1737

Greece becomes an independent country

A.D. 1896

A.D. 476

Mt. Vesuvius erupts again

A.D. 1829

Present-day Olympic games begin

THE AGE OF GREECE

Ancient Greece was an area but never one nation. The people lived in city-states that were independent and were often at war with each other. Although they were sometimes competitive, all the city-states shared the same language and customs. Because of the rugged land, most people settled in river valleys or along the coast. In time the population grew too large for the food supply, so Greek city-states began to set up colonies in other places.

Greeks sailed around the Mediterranean Sea in search of locations for new settlements.

A landless Greek could go to a colony and become a landowner. Others just wanted to go for the adventure. The colonists took a sacred flame from the hearth of the city-state. When the new colony was built and secure, it broke ties with the city-state.

Two city-states became the most important and powerful, Sparta and Athens. They were both homes to Greek citizens who spoke the same language, worshipped the same gods, and were located only one hundred miles apart. Yet life was very different in these two city-state.

MAP OF ANCIENT GREECE

Macedonia

Mt. Olympus

Sybaris

Crotone

Delphi

Carthage

Sicily

Athens

Africa

Sparta

Rhodes

Crete

Mediterranean Sea

ANCIENT GREECE

SPARTA

People in Sparta wanted order and stability. Nearly every part of life was controlled by the law, and the city-state was ruled by kings. Most Spartan citizens didn't work; they lived off the proceeds from the public lands worked by slaves and noncitizens. At about age six, children were sent to live in training barracks. Boys learned military arts and virtues like discipline, obedience, toughness, and endurance. Girls learned things they needed to know to run a home and take care of a family when they grew up. Girls also spent a lot of energy on sports and athletics. Spartans wanted girls to be strong so they would bear strong children. When boys reached the age of twenty they entered the army. They could marry, but they couldn't go live with their wives and families until age thirty. At thirty they earned the right to vote in the assembly. They served in the Spartan army until about age sixty.

Spartans ate simple foods: black broth and mush. They wore simple, plain clothing, unless going into battle, when they wore a scarlet tunic and a polished bronze helmet. Spartans were forbidden to work in stores or trade and couldn't make crafts or art because they needed to spend their efforts keeping fit and strong.

No other army ever entered Spartan territory. They were the best soldiers anywhere.

ATHENS

The citizens of Athens enjoyed freedom and liked change and creative living. They didn't work much either, having slaves do everything. Athens received profits from silver mines outside the city, so few citizens had to worry about money. Citizens were paid to serve on court juries or hold elected office. Athenians loved going to the theater to see plays and pageants. The government paid admission for the poor so everyone could attend.

Athens had an army, but it was nothing like the Spartan army. Athens also had a big navy, with more than two hundred ships. Citizens were paid to be in the navy, too.

Citizens of Athens voted for their government officials. Aristotle was an Athenian who thought that the system of voting in a democracy could become just like having a king. He said that politicians would flatter and make promises to the voters just like the members of a royal court did to a king. Then, once in office, they would serve their own interests instead of the country's. He thought laws provided a more fair system of government than election by a majority vote. Athens had a system of laws, but the citizens voted, too. They cast their votes on pieces of broken pottery. Sometimes they voted to send a politician away for several years; however, he could come back later and run for office again.

Athens was a democracy but only for free male citizens. Women couldn't vote, own property, or become citizens. They had to spend nearly all of their time inside their homes; men even did the shopping. Only people born to parents who were citizens could become citizens. At age eighteen, boys applied to become citizens of Athens. If there was doubt whether a boy was freeborn, a panel of five judges determined whether he could become a citizen or not. If it appeared he had

no right to become a citizen, the city sold him into slavery. When a boy was approved as a citizen, he went into the army and learned to fight, march, and drill. At the end of the second year the soldiers were sent out to patrol the country and live at guard posts. During the two years in the military they received a cloak but no pay. Fortunately, they didn't have to pay taxes during the two years.

Citizens of Athens were elected to many jobs. There was a treasurer of military funds, treasurers of the theater fund (all poor citizens could apply to the fund to receive money to pay for theater performances), and a superintendent of the water supply. They were elected to their positions for a term that lasted from one Panathenaea Festival to the next. The elections were held in July of each year.

In Athens there was a law that citizens who owned little property and who were physically disabled and couldn't work would receive money for their support from the public funds.

Of course there were other important city-states besides Sparta and Athens. Each was a bit different from the others. People in Sybaris, in southern Italy, put a lot of emphasis on city planning, and the citizens tried to create a pleasant place to live. Noisy businesses were prohibited inside the city and city planning created a serene, comfortable town. It was the only city-state where men ate dinner with their wives and good cooks were highly paid. People in Crotone, another city-state, valued intelligence, too, so they built a major medical school.

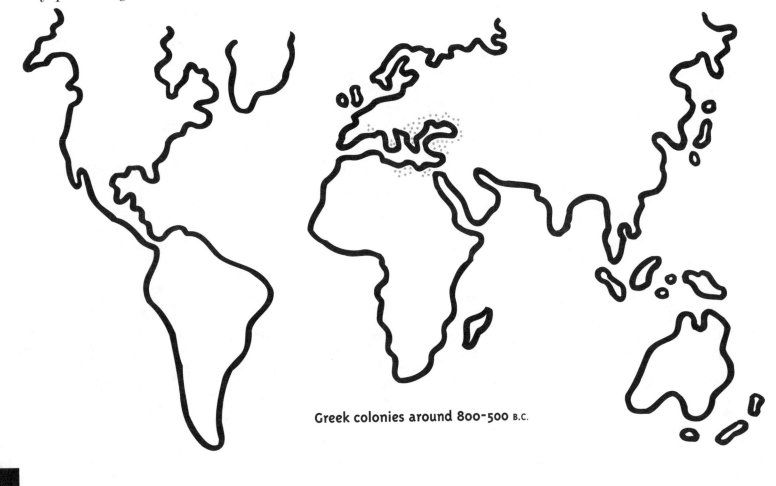

Greek colonies around 800-500 B.C.

EPIC POETRY

Not much is known about Greece before the seventh century B.C. Only legends survive from that time.

One was a long poem (called an *epic*) titled *The Iliad*, written by a poet named Homer. He designed it to be recited in public. It's about the hero Achilles who fights bravely on the side of the Greeks in the Trojan War. When his friend Patroclus is killed by the enemy, Prince Hector of Troy, Achilles gets revenge by killing Prince Hector. The poem was about the loyalty of friends to each other. Another famous epic was *The Odyssey*. It was a story about the hero Odysseus who was returning from war (he'd been gone twenty years) but had to overcome witches and giants before he made it back to the island of Ithaca. Odysseus used his clever skills to finally get home to the island of Ithaca where his wife Penelope was waiting for him. While he was away, suitors had come to Ithaca, pestering Penelope to marry one of them. Odysseus returned in a disguise, murdered the suitors, and greeted his son, Telemachus, who had grown up while he was away.

Professional reciters would tell the stories by memory to audiences who always enjoyed it when the hero was successful.

Hesiod was a Greek sheepherder who became a professional reciter of epics. He made up some of his own epics and also wrote an almanac, called *Works and Days*, which was sort of a calendar. It was full of magic and advice about saving money and working hard. Centuries later, Benjamin Franklin did the same, with *Poor Richard's Almanack*.

DRESS UP GREEK

The Greeks wore simple, loose-fitting clothing. They didn't want to restrict the body with tight garments, and they wanted to show off the grace and beauty of their physically fit bodies. It was a very warm climate, and keeping cool was more important than staying warm. Women wove the cloth in their homes. The type of yarns used in the weaving depended on the family's wealth and status. The rich wore linen; the poor and those living in the colder regions of the north wore wool. No one threw out a garment until it wore out. The Greek styles were popular for more than four hundred years and then were copied by the Romans, so there were no fashion trends to keep up with.

CHITON

Men wore a *chiton*, an oblong piece of cloth mostly worn draped around the body with a hole in one side to put one's arm through. The two ends of the open side were fastened over the other shoulder with a button or clasp. A free citizen (only boys whose parents were both citizens could become citizens) wore a chiton that fastened at both shoulders.

Workmen, artisans, and slaves wore a chiton with one hole for the left arm; the right arm and half of the chest remained uncovered. In Greece, you could tell what social class someone belonged to just by looking at his garment.

What about underwear? There wasn't any, but women did wrap a linen cloth tight around their waists to look thinner.

Chiton with a belt at the waist.

PEPLOS

A *peplos* was a long tube. The top was folded down and pinned at the shoulders.

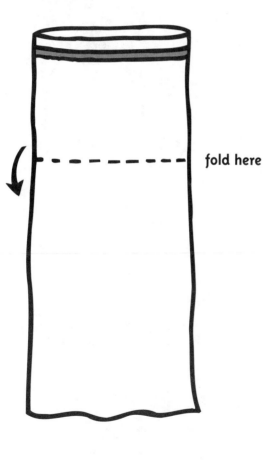

fold here

Women wore a dress called a *peplos*, which was a narrow, ankle-length tunic that doubled over at the shoulders to create a loose top that hung to the waist. It fastened at the shoulders with long straight pins. A peplos was often made in a bright color with a decorative border.

HIMATION

The *himation* was a sort of cloak in a large square shape that was worn by both men and women. How gracefully one draped one's himation showed style and social status. Tiny weights were sewn in the hem of the himation so it would drape elegantly.

Himation

SHOES

Greeks wore sandals, some with thick soles to make men taller, some with a lot of jewels for rich ladies. Greeks took off their sandals before going inside a house, but to make things even easier, they all went barefoot most of the time.

HAIR

Greek women wore simple hairstyles: long hair tied up in the back with a band that crossed the brow or parted in the center and pulled back into a bun. They liked curly hair and used curling irons to make pretty hairdos. They also used oils and hair dressings to style their hair.

Men wore short haircuts because long-flowing tresses could be grabbed by an enemy on the battlefield. As warfare grew less important, men allowed their hair to grow longer; sometimes it was braided and pinned up at the sides or back.

girls

boys

HATS

Queens and goddesses wore coronets or diadems; other women wore scarves, simple veils, or hairnets to hide their hair. Men seldom wore hats, but travelers wore a large-brimmed hat that looked sort of like a cowboy hat and hung on the back from a cord around the neck.

Women wore simple veils.

Travelers wore straw hats.

GREEK BEAUTY

The Greeks paid a lot of attention to how their bodies looked. To keep in shape, men worked out at the gym doing exercises, lifting weights, and swimming. Rhythm and balance were also important—a graceful walk was appreciated.

The Greeks studied the human body and came up with what they thought the perfect body should look like:

The neck should be long and powerful.

Ankles and feet should be shapely, and the small toe should be the same length as the big toe.

A man should be six times as tall as the length of his foot. A woman should be eight times as tall as the length of her foot.

Use a ruler to measure the length of your foot. Multiply it by 6 (for boys) or 8 (for girls). How do you measure up? Try measuring family members. Do you think the proportion should be different for children and adults?

The Greeks thought a man should be 6 times as tall as the length of his foot; a woman should be 8 times as tall as the length of her foot.

BIRTHSTONES

About 700 B.C. Greeks decided that stones held magic and gave each month a special stone. People with birthdays in that month or people dressing for a special festival could wear the stones of that month for extra luck and protection.

Here's a list we use today, with many of the same stones the Greeks used. What is the stone for your birth month?

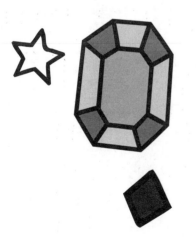

JANUARY	GARNET
FEBRUARY	AMETHYST
MARCH	AQUAMARINE
APRIL	DIAMOND
MAY	EMERALD
JUNE	PEARL
JULY	RUBY
AUGUST	PERIDOT
SEPTEMBER	SAPPHIRE
OCTOBER	OPAL
NOVEMBER	TOPAZ
DECEMBER	TURQUOISE

STONE PENDANT

Materials

Smooth stone, at least ½ inch by ½ inch

Clear fingernail polish

#18 gold-, silver-, or copper-tone wire (available in craft supply stores)

Wire cutter

Pliers

Wrap wire around a stone.

Make a necklace to wear the pendant.

You can make a clever stone pendant from any interesting smooth stone you find. Paint a coat of clear nail polish on the stone to make it shine. When it's dry, cut 1 12-inch-long piece of wire. Make a cage for the stone by wrapping the wire around the stone, using your fingers to press it to the stone. Keep wrapping until the stone is secure. Use the pliers to bend a loop at the top.

Wear the pendant on a chain or make a neck ring from wire by bending wire into a circle big enough to go around your neck comfortably. String the pendant on the wire and then twist the ends of the wire into loops at the back to interlock. You may need to string the pendant on the neck ring before bending the back loops into shape.

EATING GREEK

The first Greek families lived on small farms and grew wheat or barley, cultivated fig and olive trees, and raised pigs for meat and goats for milk used to make cheese. As the number of people increased, the hillsides were stripped of trees, which were used to build houses and trading ships and to make charcoal to use in metalworking. The soil washed away in the rain, and the hills lost soil. The sediment covered the valleys and ruined the farmland.

With so little land, the Greeks needed to grow something they could trade in exchange for the food supply they needed. Since everyone in the ancient world used oils for cooking, lighting, medicine, body oil, and perfumes, the Greeks decided to grow olive trees and make olive oil for trade. They didn't plant much else. While the people prospered for 150 years by growing olives, they quit raising livestock, wheat, and barley. Because they were even more dependent on other countries for food, they had to produce even more oil for trade. The imported grain was so valuable that it was used in bread and not fed to livestock, so the people didn't eat much meat.

The foods eaten in ancient Greece were simple, and the diet of both rich and poor

Grecians was pretty much the same. Everyone ate barley mush, barley bread, olives, figs, goat's milk cheese, salted fish, and eggs. Wealthy people ate more pork and enjoyed things like honey cakes with spices. The wealthy homes also had cooks with more time to create interesting dishes from these basic foods.

Ancient Greeks thought food and cooking was an art. Male slaves did most of the cooking, and professional cooks were hired to cook special meals. At a Greek dinner, the number of people to be seated at a table was five—never more. Greeks enjoyed conversations and thought more than five people would be too many for a good discussion.

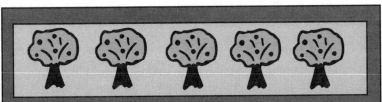

Ancient Greeks didn't eat butter; they said it was food for the barbarians. They thought butter caused disease. They preferred olive oil on bread. They liked olive oil so much that they created groves of sacred olive trees. The oil produced from the olives on these trees was given out as prizes in athletic contests. (These trees were considered so holy that if anyone dug up or cut down one of them, the person was executed.) Greeks milked goats and sheep and used the milk to make cheese. They didn't drink cow's milk.

Greeks kept wine or oil in bags made of animal skins sewn together, tied at the top, and stopped with a cork. They could take the bag along to work or when traveling because it had a strap that could be slung over the shoulder.

ASPARAGUS

The Greeks loved asparagus. They even had a saying about it. If they wanted something done in a hurry they said, "Do it in less time than it takes to cook asparagus."

4 servings

Ingredients

1 pound fresh asparagus

1 tablespoon olive or salad oil

Mayonnaise or your favorite salad dressing

Utensils

Serrated plastic knife

Large saucepan

Colander

Large bowl of cold water

✸ (Adult help suggested.)

Wash the asparagus in the sink and trim off the ends that are whitish and tough. Fill the saucepan half full of water and add the oil. Bring it to a boil on the stovetop. Add the asparagus and let it simmer for 4 minutes. Drain the asparagus in the colander, and then plunge it into the bowl of cold water to chill quickly. Drain it again and enjoy with a spoonful of mayonnaise or your favorite salad dressing.

Microwave Method: Cut the asparagus into 2-inch pieces. Put it in a 2-quart casserole with a lid. Add ¼ cup of water and microwave on high for 4 minutes. Drain in the colander, and then plunge the asparagus into the bowl of cold water to chill it quickly.

The Greeks copied the Persians' habit of lying on couches to eat meals. They ate with their fingers, wiped their mouth on pieces of bread, and washed in a small fingerbowl when the meal was over.

Asparagus grows out of the soil in early spring. You can cut asparagus from an asparagus bed for years.

SPINACH TRIANGLES

Called *spanakopita*, spinach triangles are fun to make and are just like what ancient Greek people would have purchased at the market to take home for dinner. There was no need for plates, making them the first fast-food take-out meal.

Ingredients

2 packages frozen chopped spinach

1 stick butter

3 green onions, chopped

8 ounces feta cheese

15 ounces ricotta cheese or small curd cottage cheese

3 eggs, beaten

1 or 2 tablespoons chopped parsley

1 pound frozen fillo pastry dough (found in your grocery store's frozen foods section)

Utensils

Colander

Fork

2 saucepans

Measuring spoons

Spoon

Damp towel or layer of damp paper towels

Pastry brush

Serrated plastic knife

Baking sheet, greased

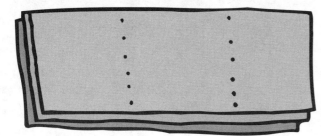

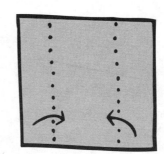

Cut fillo dough in thirds.

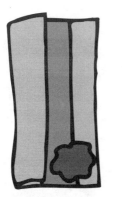

**Put filling in lower right corner.
Fold up in triangles.
Tuck edges under.**

**Fold in 1 inch along the sides of 1 piece
of dough. Brush with butter.**

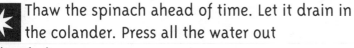

Bake until golden brown.

Thaw the spinach ahead of time. Let it drain in the colander. Press all the water out with a fork.

Heat the oven to 375° F.

Put a tablespoon of butter in the saucepan and add the onion. Stir over medium-low heat until the onion is cooked. Add the drained and squeezed spinach and simmer a few minutes. Remove the pan from the heat and stir in the feta cheese, ricotta cheese, eggs, and parsley. Mix well. Melt the rest of the butter in a pan on low heat.

Open the fillo dough and cut it into three pieces. Place a damp towel over the dough to keep it from drying out before you use it. Remove one sheet at a time. Fold in the sides about 1 inch. Brush the dough with melted butter. Place a tablespoon of spinach-cheese filling in the lower corner. Fold the dough in triangles, over and over, until you get to the end of the dough strip. Tuck the ends under. Place the triangles on the baking sheet. Bake for about 30 minutes, until they are golden brown.

MINI PIZZAS

2 servings

Greeks were the first to eat pizza, using it as a bread plate to pile food on top of. They baked thick grain mush (called *puls*) on the ashes beneath the stones in the kitchen fireplace. It made a flat bread that was the first pizza crust. We eat pizza today with a juicy layer of tomato sauce. Ancient Greeks couldn't do the same because tomatoes were grown only in the New World, and Columbus hadn't even been born yet! It was the Middle Ages before Europeans could enjoy tomatoes on their pizza.

✶ (Adult help suggested.)
Preheat oven to 350° F.

Use a pastry brush to spread a thin coat of olive oil on the open side of each muffin half. Sprinkle on the toppings: cheeses, salami, and olives. Place the pizzas on the baking sheet and bake them in the oven. Bake until the cheese melts, about ten minutes.

olives

Ingredients
1 English muffin, split open

2 tablespoons olive oil

¼ cup Cheddar, Monterey Jack, Swiss, or whatever cheese you have, grated

¼ cup sliced black olives

2 slices of salami

Anything else you like on your pizza

Utensils
Pastry brush

Cookie sheet

olive oil

cheese

salami

Olive trees take thirty years to mature and bear olives, but they live for two hundred years. They're very hard to sprout from seeds so most farmers grow them from pieces cut off live trees. Olives are grown around the Mediterranean Sea and also in California. Most olives in the United States come from California and are black. But they're not that color to start with; they start out green.

Canning black olives was first practiced by a California woman, Freda Ehmann, who canned olives on her back porch. She figured out how to process green olives so they would turn black and could be kept in cans for a long time.

Factory-packed California olives are picked green and put in a lye bath with air bubbled through the tanks. (Ehmann discovered that air will cause the green olives to turn black in the lye.) Then the pits are punched out with a machine that can pit one thousand olives a minute. The olives are packed in cans and cooked at high heat to keep them from spoiling. Try a taste test with your family or friends. Taste California black olives, green Manzanilla olives (they sometimes have bits of pimento in the center), and Greek olives. Can you tell the difference among these olives when tasting them with your eyes closed? Do the Greek olives taste different? Do you prefer black olives or green olives?

After the evening meal, Greek men would hold a symposium where guests discussed different ideas, sang hymns, and drank wine until it was time to go home.

BAKED FISH IN GRAPE LEAVES

A Greek named Archestratus wrote one of the first cookbooks. His recipe for baked fish told the cook to buy fish from Byzantium, sprinkle it with marjoram (a dried herb), and wrap the fish in fig leaves. After baking, slaves should serve it on silver platters.

Utensils

Serrated plastic knife

Baking pan, greased or oiled or lined with aluminum foil

✳ (Adult help suggested.)
Preheat oven to 350° F.

Cut the fish into pieces about 1 inch square. Wash and cut the onions into ½-inch pieces. Sprinkle the marjoram, salt, and pepper on the fish pieces. Sprinkle the lemon juice over the fish, too. Spread the grape leaves open (you may want to rinse them in cold water to help open them). Place a piece of fish in the center of each leaf. Sprinkle some onion on top. Fold the leaf over the fish, tucking the sides in as you roll it up. Place the rolls in the baking pan and pour the water over them. Bake in the oven for 20 minutes.

Ingredients

5 servings

½ pound whitefish, halibut, or sole

4 green onions

½ teaspoon dried marjoram

Salt and pepper to taste

2 tablespoons lemon juice or the juice squeezed from 1 lemon

1 small jar of canned grape leaves

1 cup water

Place the fish in the center of a grape leaf.

Fold the sides and ends in and bake the fish in the leaf wrap.

28

ROASTED CHICKEN

Greeks enjoyed roasting many different birds—even peacocks! Chickens are more to our liking today.

⭐ (Adult help suggested.)
Preheat oven to 375° F. Wash the chicken and pat dry with paper towels.

Mix the olive oil, oregano, lemon juice, and salt and pepper in the bowl. Place the chicken in the mixture and turn it over until it's coated. Use a pastry brush to put some of the mixture inside the chicken, too. Place it in a baking pan and cook for 1 hour.

Ingredients

4 servings

2- to 3-pound chicken

½ cup olive oil

1 tablespoon ground oregano

2 tablespoons lemon juice

Salt and pepper to taste

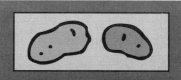

Potatoes were unknown in ancient Greece and Rome. They were first grown in the New World.

Brush chicken with olive oil and seasoning mixture before baking.

Utensils

Paper towels

Bowl or pan

Baking pan, large enough to fit chicken

Pastry Brush

SESAME CIRCLES

Greeks were the first people to make really good breads. They baked loaves, rolls, and cakes from whole wheat, rice, and barley. They added cheese, honey, milk, poppy seeds, and oil to improve the taste. When the Romans took over Greece, they enslaved Greek bakers, took them to Rome, and forced them to share their bread-baking secrets.

10-12 servings

Ingredients
Oil for baking sheet
Flour to dust work surface
1 loaf frozen bread dough, thawed
¼ cup milk
2 to 3 tablespoons sesame seeds

Utensils
Paper towel
Baking sheet
Rolling pin
Serrated plastic knife
Pastry brush

(Adult help suggested.)

Preheat oven to 425° F. Use a paper towel to spread oil evenly on the baking sheet so the breads won't stick to the pan while baking.

Dust flour on the work surface and use the rolling pin to roll out the bread dough. Flatten it to about ¼ inch thick, and then cut it into strips ½ inch wide. Piece together 2 strips to make a longer strip. Form these strips into circles on the baking sheet, overlapping the ends. Brush a little milk on the strips and sprinkle on some sesame seeds. Bake the circles for 15 minutes, until they are just golden brown.

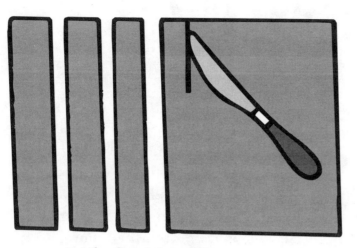

Cut the dough into strips.

Form into circles, brush with milk, and sprinkle with sesame seeds.

Cooks were highly prized in Greece. They worked for themselves and were paid to come into a home, bringing their own pots, pans, and helpers. Famous cooks could become wealthy, and their recipes couldn't be copied by anyone else for one year. After a feast, the cook could sell the leftovers in the marketplace.

GREEK SLAVES

In Athens people could buy houses, making one payment a year for five years. They didn't make many payments, but the amounts were large. Home loans had an interest rate of 12 percent a year or more. There weren't banks then, but rich people profited by lending money to others and charging interest. People would use themselves and their family as security for the loan. If they couldn't pay, the lender could take them into slavery. Other slaves were acquired from conquered lands.

Around Athens, farms that had been *mortgaged*, or had money borrowed against them, displayed stones bearing the name of the mortgage holder, who received one-sixth of each harvest from the farmer until the debt was paid.

When Solon was elected archon (one of nine judges who governed Athens), he abolished debt slavery and canceled all land debts. He did it to keep the people from revolting against the government. Too many people hadn't been able to pay for houses or land and had sold themselves into slavery in order to make the payments. Solon made new laws, and they were displayed in towns on wooden pillars. Solon was popular with the voters, but not with the wealthy lenders.

If you were wealthy in Athens, life was good. If you weren't, it was hard to get a job. That's because the wealthy people owned so many slaves. Slave owners rented their slaves to work on public works projects for the government. Some businessmen rented more than a thousand slaves to work in the government mines or to repair the roads, taking the slaves' paychecks as profit. Educated slaves worked in government offices, doing all the bookkeeping and office work. There were three hundred slaves who worked as policemen in Athens. Slaves did just about everything in Greece. That made it hard for someone who needed to work for a living to find a job.

Temple builders hired both slaves and freemen to do the work. They paid the same wages to both. Since slaves had to work no matter what, their owners kept wages low to get the work done at a very low cost. This left the freemen to work for nearly nothing, *if* they could get a job.

Since freemen could vote, why didn't they vote to end slavery? They hoped someday they'd be wealthy, too, and they wanted a chance to own slaves of their own.

In Athens in 431 B.C., there were 40,000 male citizens and 100,000 slaves; in Sparta there were 8,000 male citizens and 160,000 slaves—far more slaves than citizens. Where did all the slaves come from? Pirates and kidnappers supplied the slave markets, and prisoners of war were sold into slavery if their relatives couldn't buy them back. In all the Greek cities, unwanted or sickly babies were set out in the woods to be eaten by wolves. Slave traders snatched them up and raised them for sale.

THE ARTS

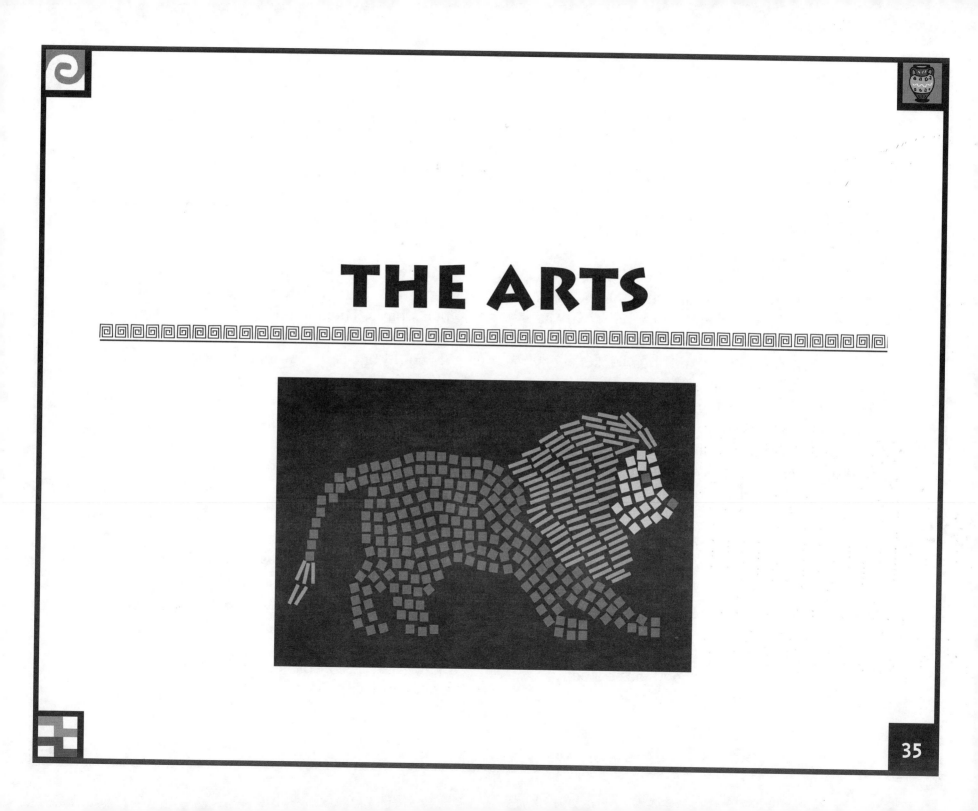

GREEK THEATER

People enjoyed watching plays in the large theaters that were built in every Greek town. Some were built below small hills; in these the audience sat in the grass. Other theaters were built from stones placed in arches and could hold thousands of viewers. People began arriving at daybreak and brought picnics with them: bread, wine to dunk it in, olives, and figs. Tickets cost money, but poor people were given the money by the government. In Athens, the theater expense was the biggest cost of the government. Sometimes the government had to spend money saved up in case of war on theater tickets because citizens would elect politicians who gave them free theater.

Each ticket was marked with the row and seat, and theater police kept people from taking the wrong seat.

Actors were always men; women were never allowed to be in plays. Men wore masks to play women's parts. The audience sat far away from the actors. Their masks were big and bright so the actors could be seen. A woman's mask was white; a man's, brown.

Gather some friends and make up a play based on one of the epics, or do as the Greeks did and make up the adventures of the gods and goddesses, who were said to live on Mount Olympus, the highest mountain in Greece. Here's a list to help keep them straight:

Zeus: father of most of the gods; he was the sky god and controlled rain and thunder

Hera: Zeus's wife and the goddess of marriage and children

Poseidon: god of earthquakes, horses, and the sea

Apollo: handsome young god of music, poetry, and medicine

Artemis: goddess of wild beasts and a huntress

Athena: war goddess and the goddess of potters, weavers, metalworkers, and teachers

Hermes: trickster god, protector of merchants and thieves; gave good luck (every house, crossroads, and marketplace displayed a stone image of Hermes for luck)

Aphrodite: goddess of beauty, laughter, and love

Pluto: Zeus's brother who lived underground and watched over the dead (it was said that the dead were witless, pale, and squeaked around in the dark)

Pan: demon that frightened animals and scared lonely travelers, he lived in the dense forests of early Greece

Dionysus: (called Bacchus by the Romans) god of drunkenness; he was a god people made up in order to have celebrations

AESOP'S FABLES

Aesop was a slave who gained his freedom from his Greek master and went to the city of Babylon. He worked there as a riddle solver for the king. He made up stories about animals that acted like people. Aesop's fables were told for centuries before anyone wrote them down.

A *fable* is a story that has a *moral*, or truth, that people can use to improve their lives. Aesop's fables are still interesting today, even though they are about twenty-six centuries old.

THE DOG AND THE MEAT

A dog was standing beside a river with a big chunk of meat in his mouth. He looked into the water and thought he saw a dog holding a bigger piece of meat. He greedily snatched for the bigger piece and dropped his own into the water. He didn't realize it was only his own reflection.

Moral: If you are too greedy you might lose what you have.

THE BOY WHO CRIED WOLF

A shepherd boy was bored, so he ran to the village screaming that a wolf was attacking his sheep. The villagers ran to help him, but he only laughed and said there was no wolf at all. He did this several times. One day a wolf came, and when he screamed for help no one went to help him. The wolf killed all his sheep.

Moral: If you tell lies, no one will believe you when you tell the truth.

Why not try making up some fables of your own?

Choose one or two animals:

Gerbil	Pigeon
Guinea pig	Crow
Goldfish	Dolphin
Earthworm	Shark
Snail	Lizard
Raccoon	Mouse

Then choose an action that results in a *moral*, or lesson about life:

"Don't sacrifice just for the sake of your looks."

"Be thankful for the things you have and do not always want more than you need."

"Beware the clever schemes of other people."

"Don't take something from someone else when you cannot even use it yourself."

"Don't feel sorry for people who find themselves in trouble because of their own foolishness."

"Once we are used to something we are no longer frightened by it."

"There is strength in working together."

MAKE A MASK

Cut holes in a paper plate for the eyes and mouth. Use markers or crayons to color the mask. Cut and glue scraps of colored paper or yarn to the mask and decorate using the cotton balls and pipe cleaners to suit the theme you've decided on.

There are two ways to use the mask. Glue the bottom of the mask to a paint-stirring stick and hold the mask up to your face while acting. Or punch three holes in the mask, at the top and on either side. Thread a piece of yarn through each hole and knot it. Tie all three strings together in the back loose enough to fit your head inside.

Materials

Paper plate

Scissors

Colored markers or crayons

Scraps of colored papers, yarns, cotton balls, and pipe cleaners

Paint stirring stick (available in paint department of hardware store)

Hole punch

Yarn

comedy mask

tragedy mask

slave mask

PANDORA'S BOX

The Greeks had many stories and poems about people, gods, and goddesses from the past. One story is about a woman named Pandora who couldn't control her curiosity and opened a box she had been forbidden to peek into. When she lifted the lid, all the bad things in the world came out, and that's how the world got sickness, greed, sadness, and more.

Make a Pandora's box of your own.

Materials

Paper

Pencil

Glue

Small cardboard box with flaps or lid to seal *or* make a box using the pattern on page 50

Draw pictures or write down things that you'd like to get rid of, put them inside the box, and glue it shut! Maybe putting things in the box will make you feel better about things you can't change, like: hunger, poverty, crime, violence, or maybe even cockroaches and head lice!

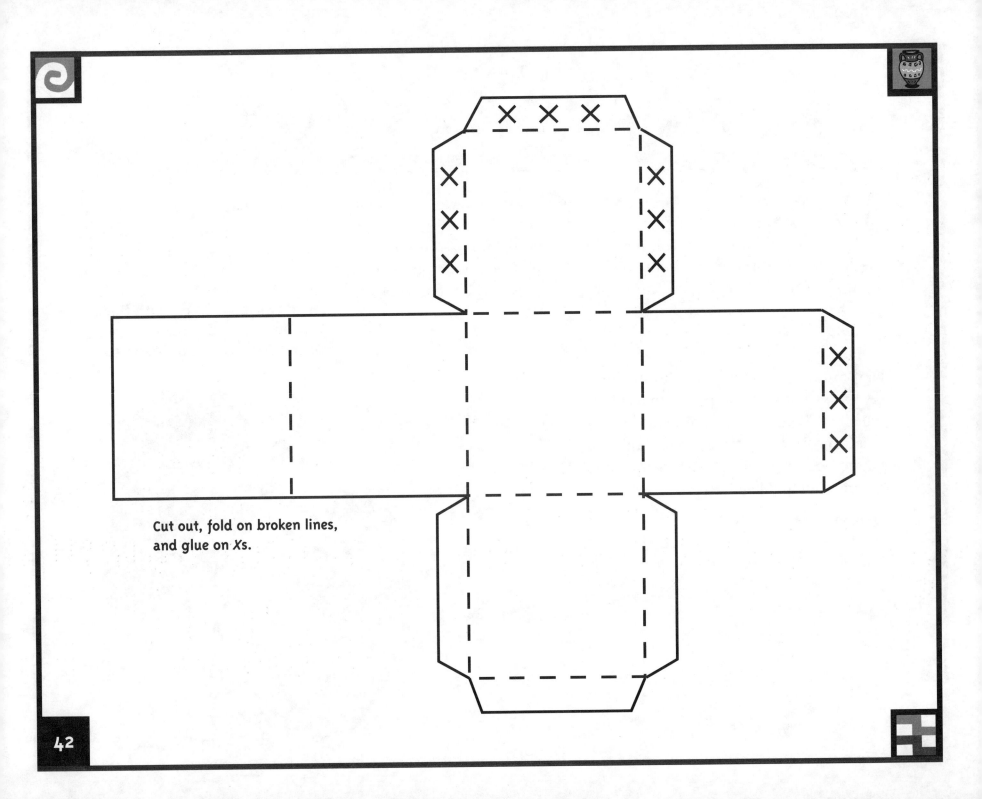

Cut out, fold on broken lines,
and glue on Xs.

SCULPT A STATUE

People made some Greek statues out of clay; they made others by carving images out of blocks of stone. Sculptors use a framework called an *armature* inside a statue to give the clay its shape. An armature will keep the figure's arms, legs, and head from falling off.

Materials

Thin, flexible wire (available at hardware stores)

Oil-based nonhard-ening modeling clay, like Plastilina

Scissors or wire cutter

Greek statues were once painted in really bright colors; some even had false eyelashes glued on. But because the statues have weathered over the centuries, they are now white.

Press bits of clay over the wire to make a figure.

★ (Adult help suggested.)
To make a small statue of a person, cut 3 pieces of wire. Make 2 pieces about 12 inches long and 1 piece 8 inches long. Bend and wrap the wire to create a stick figure, twisting the wire to hold it in place to make arms and legs and an oval for the head. Twist the ends to make rounded hands and feet.

When the figure is the size you want, begin covering the wire with pieces of clay, pressing it together around the wire with your fingertips.

Position the wire figure how you want it to stand, and complete the modeling. If you're not happy with it, pull off the clay, redo the wire, and try again!

WHAT A RELIEF!

A *bas relief* is a statue that's flat on one side so it can be part of a wall or pillar or the side of a box. Greek artists sculpted reliefs showing people, gods, goddesses, or animals.

Materials

Oil-based nonhardening modeling clay, like Plastilina

Aluminum pie pan

Tools to press designs into clay such as nails, nutshells, Popsicle stick

Plaster of Paris

Coffee can

Spoon

Water

Paper clip

Acrylic floor wax

Brush

Press modeling clay into the bottom of the pie pan until it's about ½ inch thick. Smooth the surface with your fingers. Use tools to press designs into the soft clay. Press the design; don't dig it into the clay. This way the plaster will come out easier.

Mix the plaster of Paris in the coffee can. Fill the can half full of water, and then slowly pour in dry plaster until it quits dissolving immediately in the water. When it begins to form an "island" in the water, that's enough plaster. Stir thoroughly but gently. When the plaster is getting thick, pour it over the clay in the pie pan. Bend a paper clip and insert it in the plaster, before it hardens, to make a hook for hanging your relief on the wall.

Let it sit several hours, even overnight, to become hard. Gently pop it out of the mold, and you'll see the design you made in the clay show up in relief on the plaster.

Clean up the relief with your fingers or an old toothbrush. Rub the edges smooth. Cover the relief with a coat of clear acrylic floor wax to seal it.

Modeling clay

Plaster

45

PAPER MOSAIC

In the early days of Greece, floors in houses were made of clay that was stamped or pounded to make a smooth surface. Bits of broken pottery were pushed into the clay to make a firm surface. People made the floors look nicer by pressing colored stones and special tiles into wet plaster to create elaborate mosaics. Some designs represented scenes or beautiful patterns.

Tesserae (say it: *tess-uh-ree*) are four-sided square-shaped tiles the Greeks used to make mosaics.

Materials

Colored paper in a variety of colors

Scissors

Black paper or poster board

Glue or glue stick (the kind that dries clear)

Clear adhesive paper

glue

TESSERAE (SAY IT: *TESS-UH-REE*) are four-sided square-shaped tiles the Greeks used to make mosaics.

Cut colored papers into small four-sided pieces: make squares, rectangles, and diamonds. Lay the pieces out on a piece of black paper, creating a design you like. Glue each tessera in place. Apply clear adhesive paper (like Contac) to both sides of the poster board and use it as a place mat at dinner or to make greeting cards out of.

MOM

SEED AND BEAN MOSAIC COASTER

Here's a handy and beautiful mosaic.

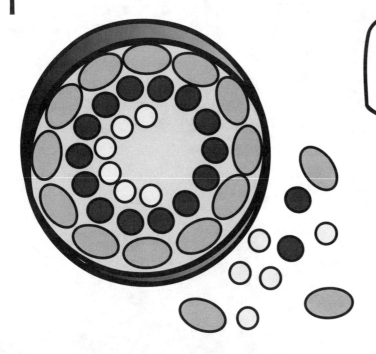

glue

Materials

Dry beans and seeds in various shapes
and colors such as navy beans, lima
beans, sunflower seeds, pumpkin seeds,
split peas, and pinto beans

Glue or glue stick
(the kind that dries clear)

Jar lid

⭐ Spread a thick layer of glue on the
inside of the jar lid. Press the beans
and seeds into the glue in an interesting
design. Let it dry. Use the coaster to keep
coffee mugs or drinking glasses from
touching the tabletop.

POTTERY

Because the number of people in Greece was growing and the forests and farmland were getting smaller, people had to think of new ways to earn money to pay for imported food and lumber. They had a lot of clay to make pots out of, so artists began making pottery. Eventually it became the best pottery in the world.

Greek pots and vases were made of red clay. The designs were etched on the sides of the pot with a tool and then painted black. Most scenery showed people doing something, like playing athletic games, working, or dancing. Much of what we know about ancient Greece comes from the detailed scenes on old pottery.

What did the Greeks use pottery for besides selling it? They gave pretty pots filled with sacred olive oil as prizes in athletic competitions. They stored wine, oil, honey, and water in pots. Figs and salted meat were also stored in big pots. Greeks served food and ate meals using pottery. Pottery placed in the graves of the dead stored supplies for the next life—food, tools, and linens. Some pots were so huge that people hid in them during the wars!

Coil the clay rolls to make a pot shape.

Smooth the rolls together with your fingertips.

Materials
Red clay (also known as terra-cotta)
Serrated plastic knife
Toothpicks
Black acrylic paint
Small paintbrush
Acrylic floor wax

Add clay rolls for handles, the top edge, and the base of the pot. Press smooth.

Use a toothpick to draw designs. Fruits, vegetables, fish, and people were popular designs in ancient Greece.

⭐ Use the knife to cut the clay into long strips. Roll each strip between your palms to make a long, thin snake of clay. Using your fingertips, gently press the rolls flat so the sides are smooth. Coil each clay snake to make a pot. When you are finished coiling one strip of clay, add a second by pressing two ends together and smoothing them with your finger or the edge of the plastic knife. Roll another thick piece of clay and coil it at the bottom of the pot for a base. Make another clay roll for the top edge of the pot, and make one or two for

handles. Wet the ends of the clay pieces and press them in place on the pot.

Before the clay hardens, use a toothpick to press the outline of a design on the sides of the pot. Make simple designs at first; make more complicated ones as you get better at it. Let the clay harden or, with the help of an adult, bake the clay pot as directed on the package. Finish the pot by painting the design within the outlines with black paint. When it's completely dry, apply a coat of shiny varnish (acrylic floor wax works well) to the outside of the pot to make it glisten.

LEARNING

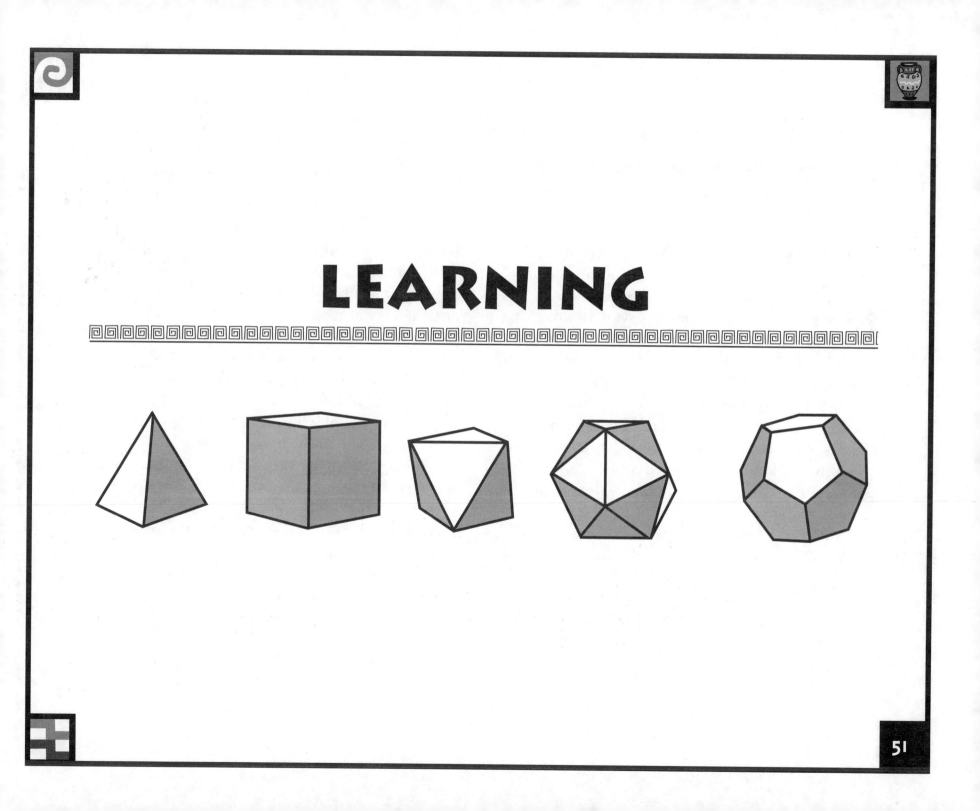

READING AND WRITING

The ancient Greeks traded with the Phoenicians and began to use their alphabet for writing. It was a big improvement over using hieroglyphic writing, which uses pictures instead of letters. With hieroglyphics it took years of experience to understand what the symbols stood for, so it was hard to learn to read until one was grown up. For the first time in history, about 1050 B.C., words could be written down just as they sounded when spoken. Also, for the first time, children could be taught to read before they learned other skills. Using hieroglyphics limited reading to older people who had learned what all the pictures meant. An alphabet, with symbols representing sounds instead of things, meant that people could write down ideas, not just lists of objects or events—words could mean something invisible or abstract.

The Phoenicians developed the alphabet, but they didn't use vowels. It was hard to tell words apart without them. For example, vowels make all the difference in *sang*, *sing*, *song*, and *sung*. How could we communicate without them? Not too well! (That would be *Nt t wll!*) The Greeks used the Phoenician alphabet but added *a*, *e*, *i*, *o*, and *u*.

Greeks used the new alphabet to write about subjects that no one had written about before, such as space, time, motion, change, quality, and more. Written down, ideas were passed on to many more people; they spread and grew.

Writing was a very important part of Greek democracy. People wrote and read information that helped them make decisions about how to vote in elections. They could read laws and books and then write down the names of the people they wanted to vote for.

The word *alphabet* comes from the first two letters of the Greek alphabet: *alph*a and *beta*. Here's what the early Greek alphabet looked like:

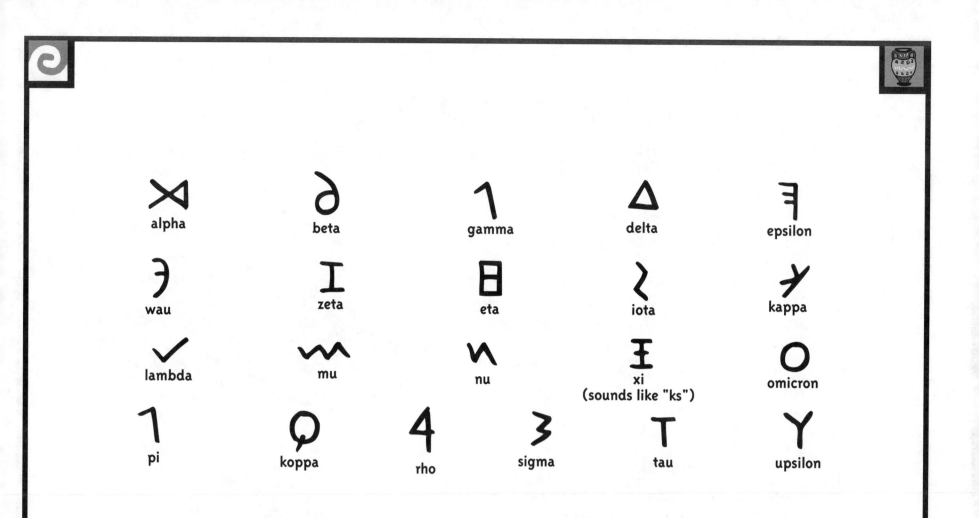

alpha   beta   gamma   delta   epsilon

wau   zeta   eta   iota   kappa

lambda   mu   nu   xi (sounds like "ks")   omicron

pi   koppa   rho   sigma   tau   upsilon

After the Romans took control of Greece, about 146 B.C., they borrowed the Greek alphabet. They kept the same letters and order, but changed the names of the letters. *Alpha* became *A*, *beta* became *B*, *gamma* became *C*, and *delta* became *D*.

Our American English alphabet is based almost exactly on the Roman alphabet. The letters *J*, *U*, and *W* were added in the Middle Ages. *U* and *W* are variations of *V*. That's why they're placed beside it in the alphabet.

CLAY TABLET

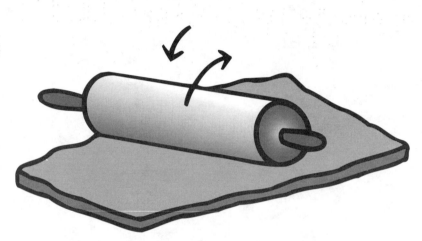

It's a good thing there was so much clay in Greece because the Greeks needed something to write on. They didn't have papyrus like the Egyptians, and they hadn't learned to make paper from rags like the Chinese. Scribes marked clay tablets with things they wanted to keep a record of. Business records were kept on tablets only as long as needed, so most weren't baked to save them. Tablets, whether baked or not, could survive if they were in a house fire, and the clay baked to harden and preserve it. Here's a fun way to practice writing, and when you're finished, you can eat the tablets!

Materials

1 roll of refrigerated sugar cookie or peanut butter cookie dough

Flour to dust the work surface

Rolling pin

Serrated plastic knife

Cookie sheet

Popsicle stick, plastic toothpick, or paper clip *or* small plastic alphabet letters

★ (Adult help suggested.)
Dust the work surface with flour to keep the dough from sticking. Roll the dough out to about ¼ inch thickness. Cut tablet shapes about 4 inches wide and 6 inches long (or any size you want). Lay the tablets on the cookie sheet and inscribe a message in the dough using a clean Popsicle stick, toothpick, or paper clip or using plastic alphabet letters.

Bake in oven as directed on the cookie dough package.

Hypatia was a woman teacher at the Alexandria library. In A.D. 415 a riot broke out in the streets. Christian monks dragged her off her chariot and killed her because her teachings didn't follow Christianity.

The library at Alexandria, a Greek city in Egypt, was huge. There were hundreds of thousands of scrolls, maybe as many as half a million. An army of copyists made copies of all Greek writings and as many books from the rest of the world as possible. The library's goal was to have a copy of every book ever written. Books were seized from trading ships in port and copied. City-states couldn't get corn during a famine until they supplied books and plays to the library.

What happened to the library? At least twice, parts of it caught fire and in A.D. 646 Arab invaders destroyed it and all books that didn't teach the religion of Islam. Scrolls were taken to the public baths and burned to heat the water for several months.

NUMBERS ARE EVERYTHING!

In about 600 B.C., the Greeks began studying numbers. Pythagoras was a mathematician, and his followers called themselves Pythagoreans. They devoted their lives to studying math. They believed that math was the basis for all things in life.

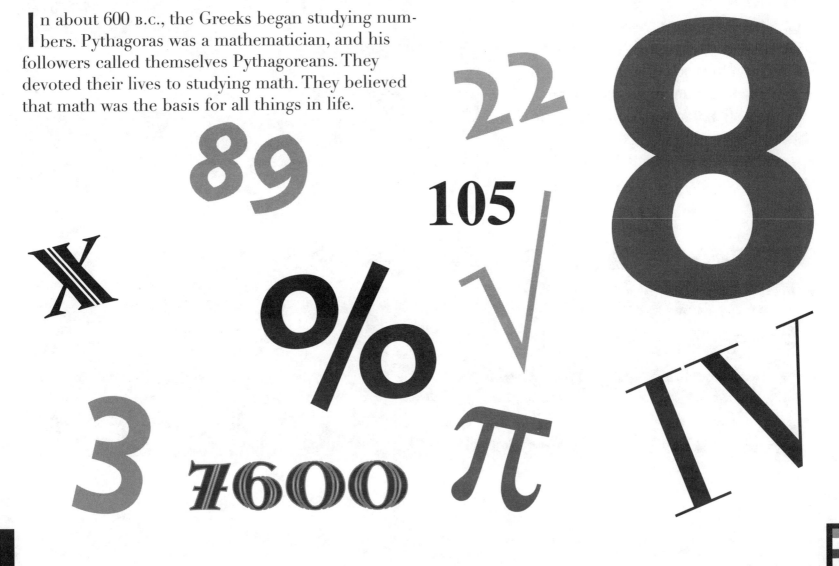

TRIANGULAR NUMBERS

Pythagoreans studied the series of numbers they called *triangular numbers*. They laid the numbers out in rows of beans or stones and saw that they always formed triangles. Try it yourself with a sack of dry beans. Can you find a number that proves the Pythagoreans wrong?

Triangular numbers

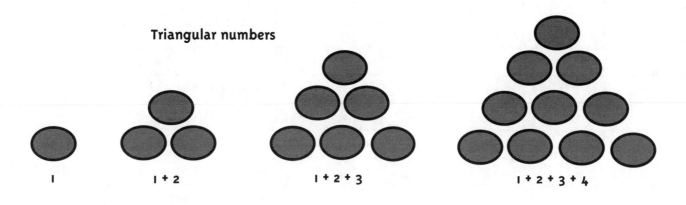

I   I + 2   I + 2 + 3   I + 2 + 3 + 4

SIEVE OF ERATOSTHENES

Another mathematician, named Eratosthenes, discovered what he called *prime number*s. These are numbers that can't be divided evenly (without a remainder) by any other number. You can make up a sieve of Eratosthenes to see if he was right.

On a sheet of paper, write the numbers from 1 to 100. Cross out all numbers that can be evenly divided by 2. Then cross out all that can be evenly divided by 3. Cross out any numbers that can be evenly divided by 5. The numbers that are left are called prime numbers. They can only be evenly divided by themselves and the number 1. Mathematicians still work with prime numbers today.

1	2	3	4	5	6	7	8	9	10
11	12	13	14	15	16	17	18	19	20
21	22	23	24	25	26	27	28	29	30
31	32	33	34	35	36	37	38	39	40
41	42	43	44	45	46	47	48	49	50
51	52	53	54	55	56	57	58	59	60
61	62	63	64	65	66	67	68	69	70
71	72	73	74	75	76	77	78	79	80
81	82	83	84	85	86	87	88	89	90
91	92	93	94	95	96	97	98	99	100

Make a chart to 100.

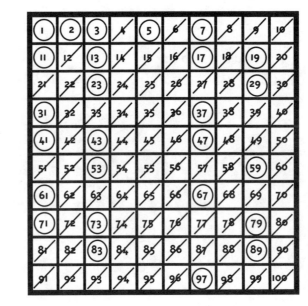

To make a sieve of Eratosthenes, cross out all numbers that can be divided by 2. Cross out all that can be divided by 3 or 5. Those left are *prime* numbers.

MAGIC SQUARE

The magic square uses all nine numbers below ten. It was a source of wonder for centuries—and still surprises us.

Add the sum of three numbers in any direction and you'll always come up with the same answer: 15. Try it with a friend!

The Greeks didn't know the idea of *zero* in math. Zero was invented by the Hindus of India over two thousand years ago. Without zero, it was difficult to do arithmetic quickly. The Greeks couldn't develop the idea of zero because they believed that it was impossible for 'nothing' or 'nonbeing' to exist. If zero represented 'nothing,' how could it exist? It was a good topic for a symposium, which the Greeks enjoyed after dinner.

4	9	2
3	5	7
8	1	6

Magic Square
Add these numbers in any direction.
The answer will always be 15.

PLATONIC BODIES

The Pythagoreans discovered that there were four figures that had all sides and angles equal. They called them the *Platonic bodies*, after Plato, a famous thinker and teacher in Greece. Follow the diagrams to trace and cut out the figures. Fold each figure on every dashed line, and fold the edge flaps (marked with *X*s) in and glue.

The Greeks discovered something they called *pi*, which can be used in math to figure out how big to make a circle. Pi is always the same, 3.14. If you want to make a circle with a 2-foot circumference (distance around the outside edge), you can figure out the diameter (width) of the circle by using pi. Divide 2 feet (or 24 inches) by 3.14, which equals 7.64 (or just over 7½). That means if you make the circle 7½ inches across, it will be about 24 inches around. Pretty tricky!

Greeks thought the number 4 was very special. There are four seasons, four directions, and four basic substances: earth, air, fire, and water. They also classified matter as dry, wet, cold, or hot—four more!

The five Platonic bodies.

 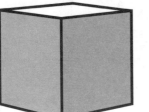   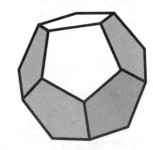

Pyramid	Cube	Octahedron	Dodecahedron	Icosahedron
4 sides	6 sides	8 sides	12 sides	20 sides

Fold on broken lines.
Glue flaps at *X*s.

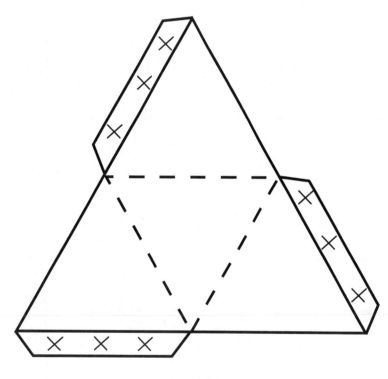

Pyramid
4 sides

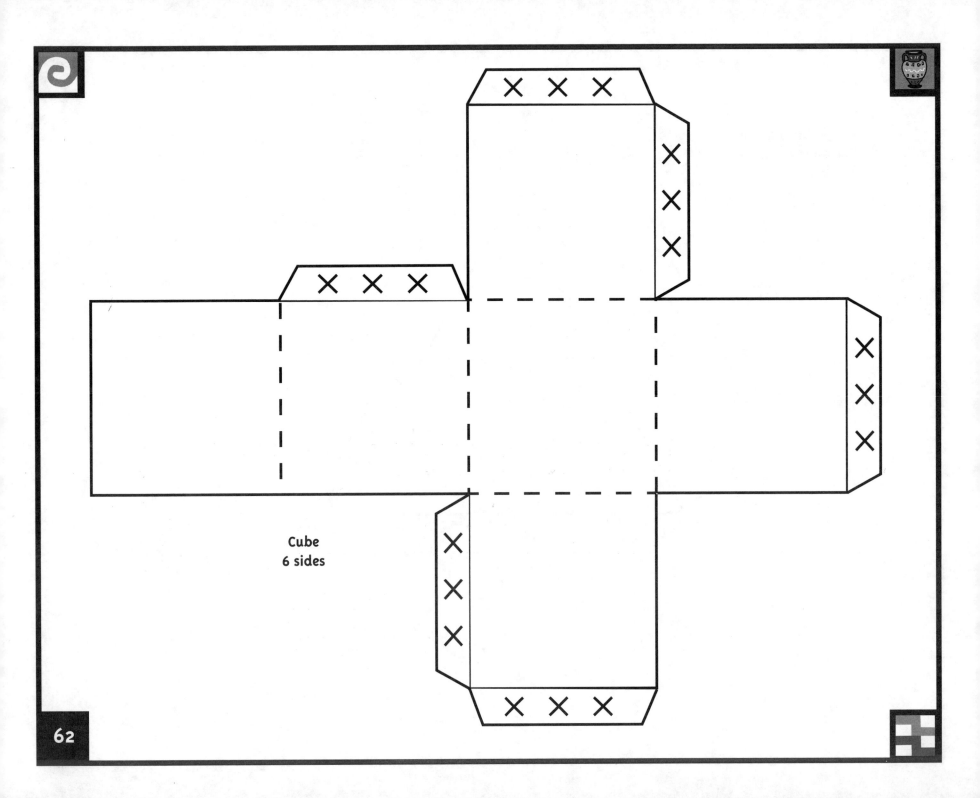

Cube
6 sides

62

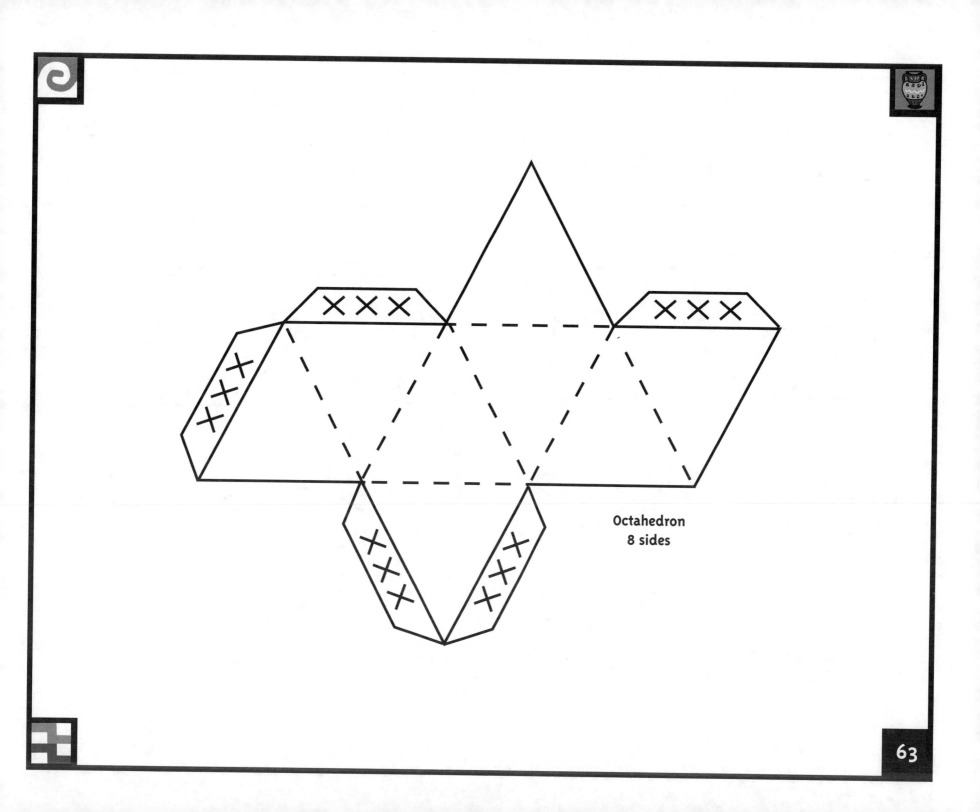

Octahedron
8 sides

Dodecahedron
12 sides

part A

part B

Attach to B here

Attach to A here

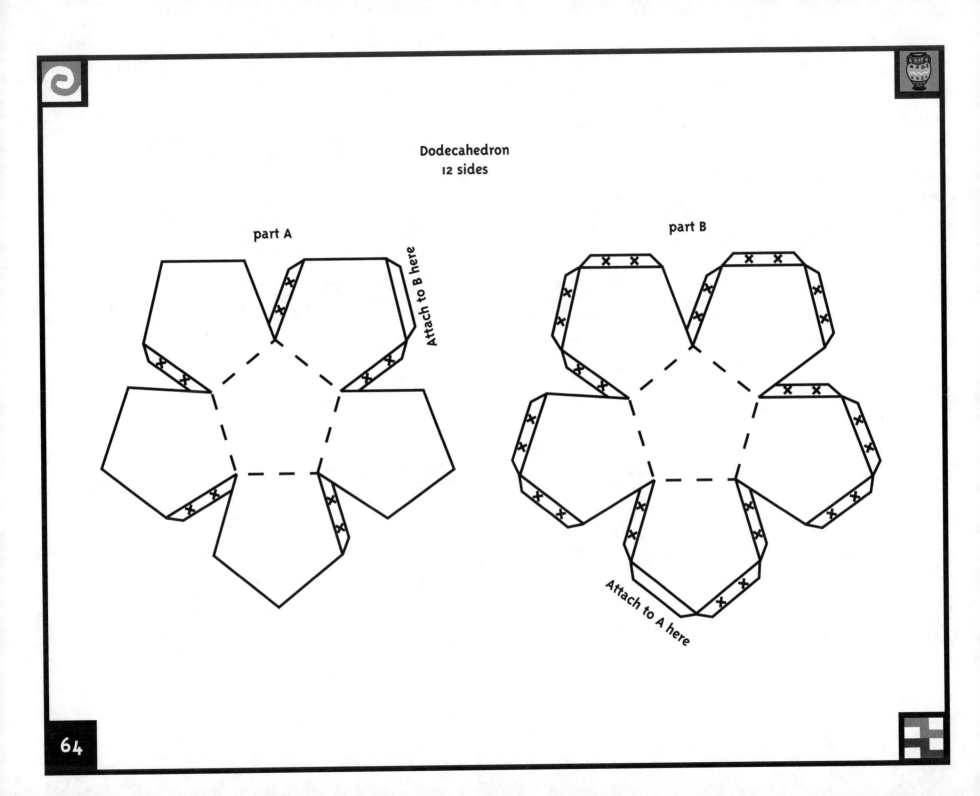

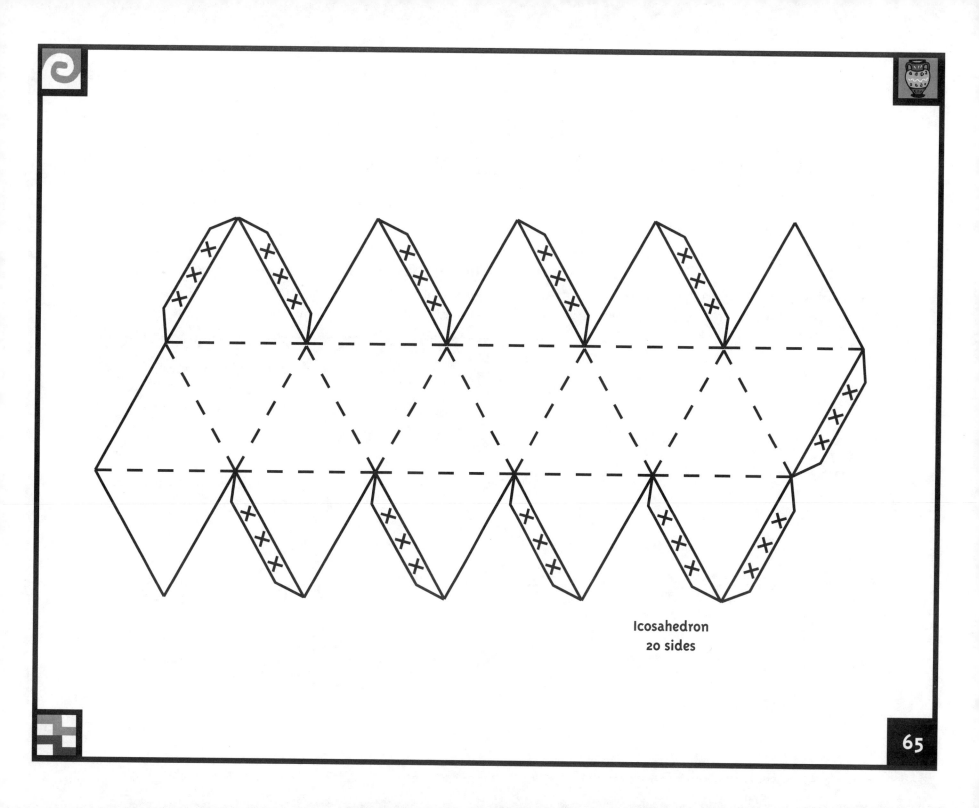

Icosahedron
20 sides

MAGIC PENTACLE

Greek mathematicians also discovered the *pentagon*, a five-sided shape. That helped them make up a *pentacle*, which is a five-pointed star (say it: pen-tuh-cul). The Pythagoreans used the pentacle as their secret sign to each other. People thought the star was a symbol that would keep evil from passing by and decorated their doorways with it. They studied the pentacle because it could be made with a "never-ending" line. Try drawing a pentacle on paper without lifting your pencil off the paper. Notice that the outside of the pentacle forms a pentagon and so does the inside of the pentacle. Clever, huh?

> The word *geometry* means "measure the earth" in Greek. The Greeks thought it up as a way to measure things using measurements, angles, and mathematical formulas.

Draw a pentacle in one line by not lifting the pencil from the paper. When you get to 5 draw a line back to 1 to complete the figure.

The outside and inside of the pentacle are both pentagons.

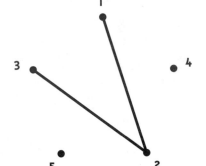

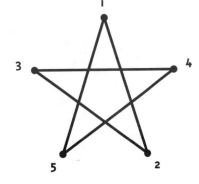

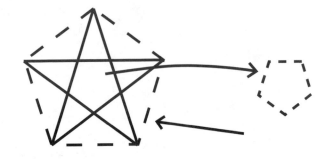

MAKE A GLOBE

Thales was a philosopher who thought the earth was a flat disc floating on water. He also believed that everything was alive. He proved it by showing how bits of iron are attracted to a magnet. Try picking up a paper clip with a magnet. Because it moves toward the magnet, is it alive?

Pythagoras was one of the first scientists to realize the earth was a sphere and not flat. The earth isn't exactly round; it's a sphere, because it isn't exactly the same all around.

Materials

Round balloon

Newspaper

1 cup flour

About 2 cups water

Pie pan or shallow bowl

Spoon

Felt tip marker

Blue, green, and brown paint

Paintbrush

Paper clip

Thread

Masking tape

To hang, bend a paper clip and insert it in a slit cut at the top of the globe. Use tape to close the slit. Tie thread to the wire loop and tape the other end to the ceiling to suspend your globe.

 Blow up the balloon and knot the end. Tear the newspaper into strips about 2 inches by 3 inches width in size. Make a pile of about 50 strips.

Mix the flour and water in the pie pan or shallow bowl, stirring and adding more water until it's like thin pancake batter. This is called papier-mâché. Dip each strip into the papier-mâché, pull it through your fingers to take off the excess paste, and press it gently onto the balloon. Cover the balloon with strips, layering the edges of the strips on top of each other. Cover the balloon with a layer at least three strips thick. Be sure the knotted end is covered with strips, too. Let it dry overnight.

When the papier-mâché is dry, sketch in the continents and oceans of the world with a marker. Use the blue paint for the oceans and the green and brown for the continents. You can hang your globe by cutting a small slit in its top and inserting a bent paper clip. Use thread and tape to suspend it from your ceiling.

NIGHT AND DAY

Once you have a spherical earth model, it's easy to see how the movement of the earth creates night and day. Use a flashlight to represent the sun, and rotate the earth model in your hand. As the earth moves, some parts move into the light as others move away. That's what makes our day and night.

Materials

Papier-mâché globe

Flashlight

Orange

Skewer

★ Demonstrate a solar eclipse. Put the skewer through the orange. Hold it between the globe and the flashlight. The orange represents the moon when it passes between the sun and the earth, causing a solar eclipse.

Anaxagoras, a Greek philosopher, heard that a shooting star had landed on earth. He took an expedition to Anatolia (part of Turkey today) to investigate the report. He examined the remains and decided that the stars, including the moon, were made of rock. Most Greek people believed that the stars were sacred holy beings. Anaxagoras was almost killed because he argued that they were made of rock.

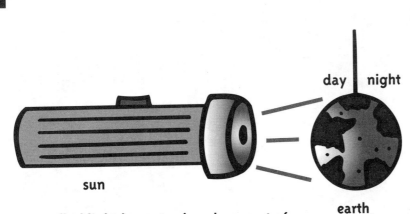

day | night

sun

earth

Use a flashlight beam to show how part of the earth is in darkness when part is in the sun's light.

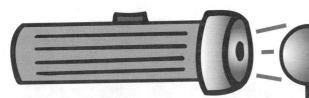

An orange stuck on a skewer shows what happens when the moon eclipses the sun.

Public speaking was the key to success in Greece. Pupils learned in school how to debate and how to argue in defense of their opinions. *Sophists* were professional teachers who charged for lessons in debate.

MAKE A CONSTELLARIUM

Greek astronomers studied the night sky. They charted more than eight hundred stars. They designed a *planetarium* to study the stars. It's a sphere of the heavens with models of the sun, moon, earth, and other planets.

You can learn some of the shapes of the constellations. *Constellations* are the patterns different groups of stars make in the night sky. Because the earth is always moving (rotating and moving around the sun), the constellations appear in different places at different times during the night and during different seasons.

Materials
Cardboard tube (from a roll of toilet paper or paper towels)
Black construction paper
Pencil
Scissors
Rubber band
Flashlight

Place one end of the cardboard tube on top of the construction paper. Draw a circle about 1 inch wider all around the tube. Cut this circle out. Wrap the paper over one end of the tube, folding and creasing it to fit, and fasten it in place with the rubber band. Use the pencil point to punch holes in the black paper to match a constellation.

When you hold the flashlight inside the tube and turn it on, your holes or stars will light up.

After you've learned a constellation or two, go out at night and see if you can locate them in the night sky.

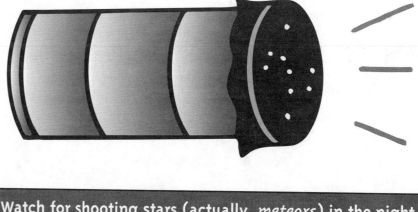

Watch for shooting stars (actually, *meteors*) in the night sky. August and November are the best viewing months.

PLANETARY MODEL

Ancient Greeks thought all the planets traveled around the earth, but today we know they all circle the sun.

Materials

Serrated plastic knife

Plastic foam balls: 1 ½-inch, 4 1-inch, 2 2-inch, 2 3-inch, 1 6-inch (or similar sizes)

Wooden skewers

Paper

Straight pins

⭐ Use the knife to trim one side off the largest ball so it is flat on one side. That will make it sit on a tabletop without rolling. This will be the sun.

Use the chart to position the planets around the sun, poking skewers into each ball and into the sun. You may need to break some of the skewers to shorten them.

Write the names of the planets on paper labels and use straight pins to fasten the labels to the planets.

½-inch ball = Pluto
1-inch ball = Mercury
　　　　　　Earth
　　　　　　Venus
　　　　　　Mars
2-inch ball = Uranus
　　　　　　Neptune
3-inch ball = Jupiter
　　　　　　Saturn
6-inch ball = Sun

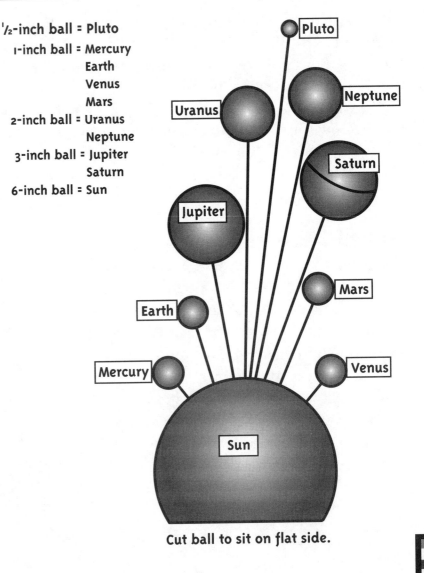

Cut ball to sit on flat side.

SOLAR SYSTEM MOBILE

Paint the balls different colors. It's easy if you poke a skewer in each ball and push the skewer into an upturned egg carton that contains the paints. Let them dry on the skewers.

Remove the balls from the skewers. Tie a three-foot-long section of thread around the thumbtacks (wrap it around the tack head several times and push it securely into the ball). Use the chart to position the planets so they are in the proper places in relation to each other and in the order shown. Adjust the length of the threads as needed. Hang the planets from your ceiling with masking tape.

To make it even more interesting, cut out tiny silver stars from foil and hang them in the solar system, too.

Want to go further? Add small balls or beads hung beside the planets to represent those that have moons. Look at the list for information.

Materials

Plastic foam balls: 1 ½-inch, 4 1-inch, 2 2-inch, 2 3-inch, 1 6-inch

Tempera or acrylic paints

Paintbrush

10 wooden skewers

Egg carton

10 thumbtacks

Scissors

Black sewing thread

Masking tape

Aluminum foil

Number of Satellites or Moons Surrounding Planets in Our Solar System

Earth: 1

Mercury: 0

Venus: 0

Mars: 2

Jupiter: 12

Saturn: 10

Uranus: 5

Neptune: 2

Pluto: 0

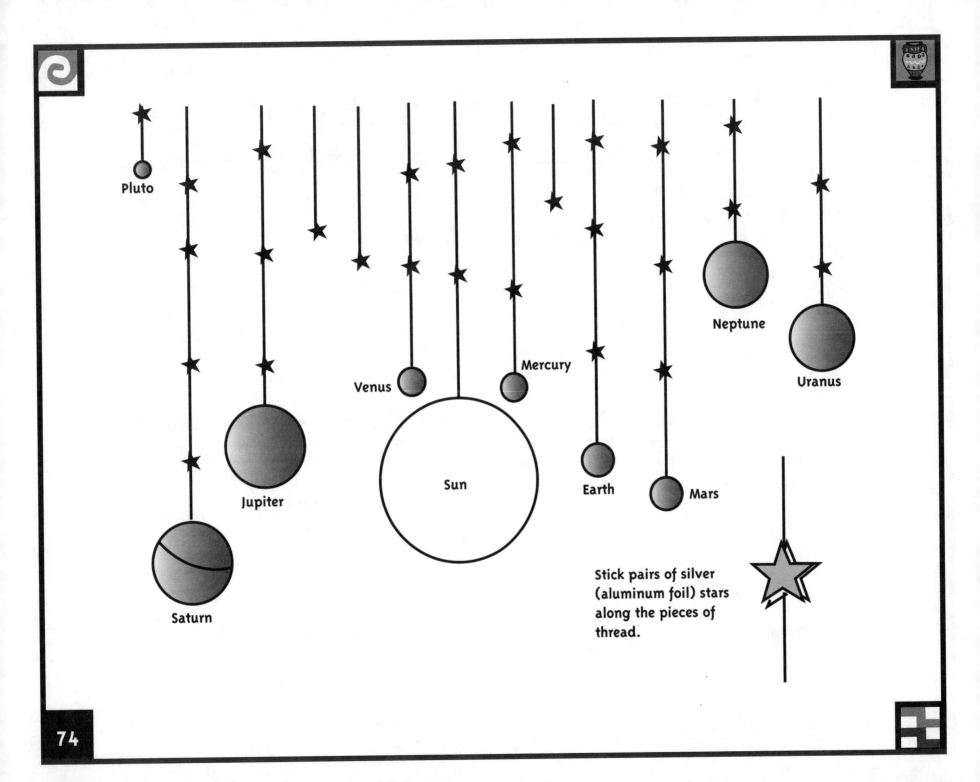

Pluto

Neptune

Uranus

Venus

Mercury

Sun

Earth

Mars

Jupiter

Saturn

Stick pairs of silver (aluminum foil) stars along the pieces of thread.

THE SECRET OF THE MOVING COIN

Ancient Greeks studied *refraction*, which is the way rays of light change when they pass from one thing to another that's made of different material. We say the materials are of different *density*. Cliomedes (A.D. 1) showed how this works with a pan of water. Try it yourself, or better yet show off for your family or friends. No one will believe their eyes!

Materials
Cake baking pan with straight-up sides

Coin

Pitcher of water

Add water, and the coin appears to have moved.

Place coin next to the pan's side.

Place the coin in the pan so the edge touches the side of the pan. Stand so that when you look at the pan, the coin is hidden by the side of the pan. Slowly pour water into the pan while you remain standing in the same spot. As you pour in the water,

the coin appears to move to the center of the pan so you can see it.

Did the coin really move? Of course not. The light rays on the coin were *distorted*, or bent, as they passed through the water, making the image appear in a different position.

SPECIFIC GRAVITY

A Greek mathematician named Archimedes was called in by a wealthy man who thought he'd been cheated. The man showed Archimedes a golden crown he suspected was made of cheaper silver and only coated with gold. The wealthy man wanted to know if Archimedes could prove the crown wasn't pure gold without damaging it.

Archimedes thought it over, and while he was sitting in the public baths the idea came to him. He noticed that as more of his body went into the bath, more of the water ran over the top. He rushed home shouting, "Eureka!" (which means "I have found it!" in Greek).

Try his experiment yourself.

Materials

Postal scale

4 quarters

5 chocolate kiss candies

Glass jar

Water

Tape or marker

Use a postal scale to prove that the 4 quarters weigh 1 ounce. The 5 candies weigh 1 ounce, too.

Fill a glass jar half full of water. Mark the level of the water with tape or a marker. Drop the quarters in the water and mark the new water level. Take the quarters out and drop the candy in the water again; mark the new water level. You'll see that the water levels are different. The coins and the candies both weigh the same (1 ounce), but the candies have more mass and they displaced more water. It proves that items with the same weight can be of different size. Some substances are heavier than others.

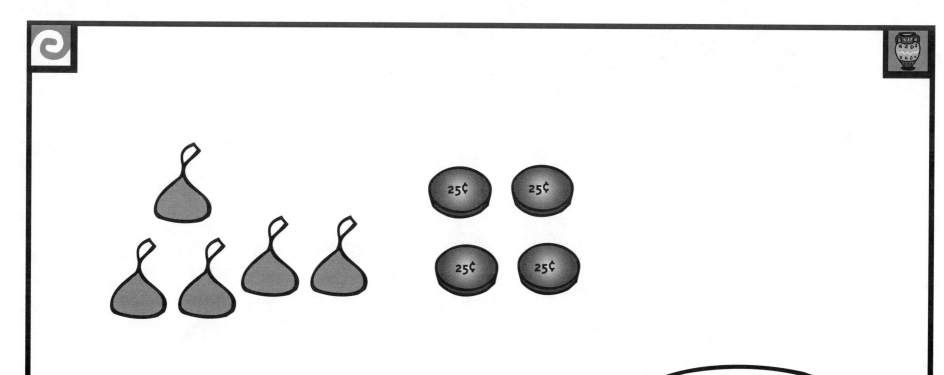

Back to Archimedes and the crown. He weighed the crown, and then he formed a piece of gold and a piece of silver, both with the same weight. He put all three in the same amount of water and saw that they had different densities. The gold piece displaced less water than the silver, because gold is denser than silver. He tested the crown and it failed to displace the same amount of water as the solid gold piece. He proved the crown was made of a substance that had a lower specific weight than real gold.

Archimedes wrote it all down, but he didn't say if the wealthy man got a refund or not.

with candies

with coins

original water level

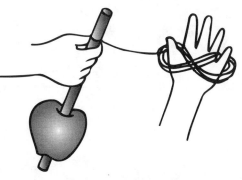

SPINNING AND WEAVING

Many slave women and children in ancient Greece had to work in the fields or at the market, but if they belonged to a wealthy family in town, they worked in the house. They were in a nice safe place, out of the sun and heat, but there was always a lot of spinning and weaving to do. Women and children did all the spinning and weaving to make the clothing, towels, bedding, and curtains for the family or to sell in the market. Families measured their wealth by how much cloth they owned and how fine it was. Most of the yarn they made was from linen or wool, but the richest women spun the finest threads; sometimes they even dipped the cloth in gold!

SPIN SOME COTTON

Materials

3 cotton balls or cotton from pill bottles

Pull a cotton ball apart.

Roll it with the palms of your hands to make a thin rope called *roving*.

To spin in the ancient style, take a small bunch of cotton fibers and pull it apart a little so it's long and loose. Roll one end down your thigh with the flat of your hand while holding onto the other end. This motion is called *spinning*. Thick yarns like the one you just spun are called *roving*.

The yarn will get longer as you continue spinning. It curls up and wraps around itself because the fibers get twisted during the spinning. When you get close to the end of the first cotton ball, start a second one and twist the end of one with the end of the new one to continue.

Ancient spinners figured out how to keep the yarn from snarling into loops and knots. They used a tool called a *spindle*. A spindle is a stick about a foot long. The end of the thread is wrapped around the stick as it's spun. By turning the spindle, the yarn can be wound and straightened as it's being spun.

But if a spinner holds the spindle, it's hard to pull and twist the fibers using only one hand. Spinners figured out that if they dropped the spindle and let it dangle from the yarn, both hands would be free to roll the fibers together. The spindle dangles and winds the yarn up on its own. Spinners would let it spin until the yarn was so long the spindle touched the ground, and then they stopped and wound the new yarn around the spindle and started over.

It wasn't until the year A.D. 1000 that the spinning wheel was invented in India. Until then, if anyone wanted clothes (or towels or bedsheets) someone had to spin the yarn on a spindle for weaving or knitting.

MAKE AND USE A DROP SPINDLE

Y̲ou don't need roving in order to try out the spindle. Use two different colors of 4-ply yarn to see how the fibers twist together to make yarn.

Materials

1 10-inch wooden dowel, $^3/_8$ inch in diameter

Apple

2 skeins of contrasting colored 4-ply yarn

1   2

Make the hitch.

3   Loop hitch over the end of the dowel and pull to secure.

★ To make the spindle, push the dowel all the way through the center of the apple, letting 1 inch protrude below.

Make a *leader* by using a piece of yarn about 2 yards long. Tie it to the dowel directly above the apple. Wind about 12 inches of yarn leader around the dowel above the apple. Loop the yarn down below the apple and around the dowel that sticks out at the bottom of the apple. Take the yarn back up to the top of the dowel and make a simple hitch to secure it (see illustration).

Lay the ends of the yarn of the two colors you will spin together over the back of your left hand, unraveling the ends a few inches. With the ends held between your thumb and finger, you're ready to spin.

Hold the end of the leader yarn in your left hand, laying it right on top of the two colored yarns. With your right hand, give the spindle a twirl so it spins clockwise. Let it spin around and watch how the leader yarn twists up. As it twists up, it will catch in the ends of the other two yarns. You may have to help it a bit, rolling the ends together with your fingers.

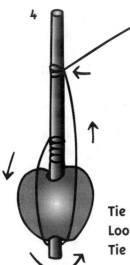

The twisting action of the yarn pulls the two colors of yarn together, spinning them into a new two-color yarn.

Tie one end of the yarn to the dowel. Loop it under the apple and back up. Tie in a hitch.

With your right hand, grasp the top of the dowel and give it a strong clockwise turn, flicking it like it was a top. As the dowel turns and drops free, the leader yarn twists. The twist travels up the yarn to your hand and catches the ends of the roving yarn, pulling it into the twist. Control the twist with your thumb and finger, not letting the two yarns unwind. Keep stopping and twirling the spindle so it never spins backward, as you pinch and pull the two yarns together through your fingers. It takes a bit of practice, but it really works.

After you've got about a foot of two-color yarn spun, wrap it around your thumb and little finger in a figure 8, so it won't unwind.

Unhitch the leader thread at the top of the spindle, and wrap the yarn you've just spun around the spindle (above the apple). Use the last part of it to be the loop at the bottom of the apple, and hitch it again at the top of the spindle. This isn't easy, but if you can keep up the rhythm-pinching, pulling, and letting go and then stopping whenever you need to spin the spindle, you'll get it to work. As you spin, the spindle will drop closer to the floor. Before it touches the floor, stop spinning and wind the yarn around the dowel. Don't let the yarn untwist from the dowel. The yarns will try to unwind at first, but eventually they'll stay twisted together. When the spindle is full of yarn, unwind the yarn and roll it into a ball.

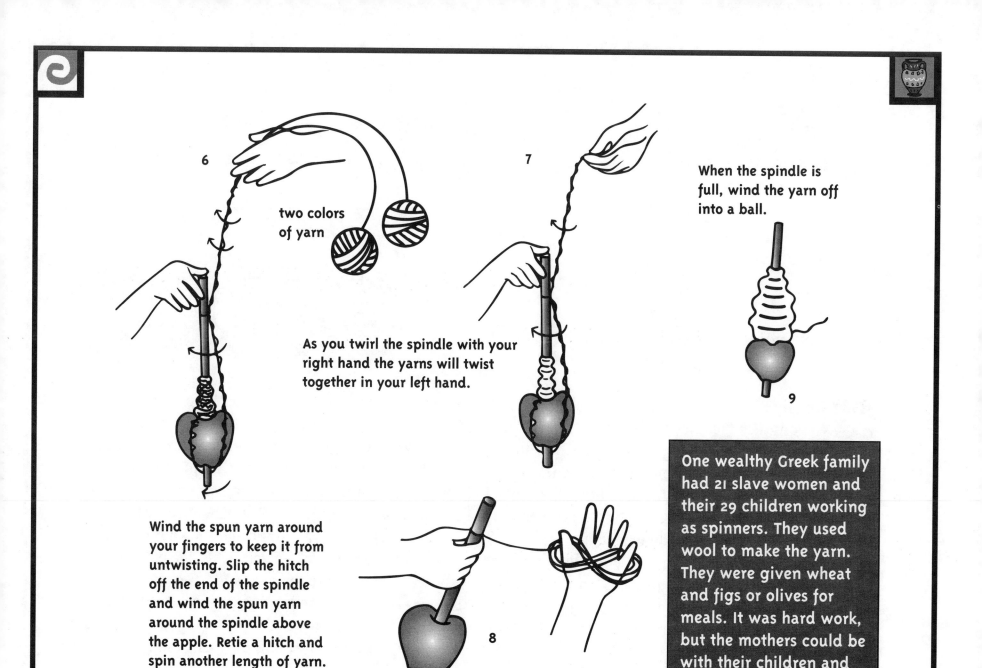

6

two colors of yarn

As you twirl the spindle with your right hand the yarns will twist together in your left hand.

Wind the spun yarn around your fingers to keep it from untwisting. Slip the hitch off the end of the spindle and wind the spun yarn around the spindle above the apple. Retie a hitch and spin another length of yarn.

7

When the spindle is full, wind the yarn off into a ball.

9

8

One wealthy Greek family had 21 slave women and their 29 children working as spinners. They used wool to make the yarn. They were given wheat and figs or olives for meals. It was hard work, but the mothers could be with their children and they got to work indoors.

WEAVE A ROUND MAT

Materials

Cardboard circle from pizza or heavyweight paper plate

Ruler

Pencil

Scissors

Yarn in several colors (about 12 yards altogether)

Popsicle stick

Greeks wrote on rolls of *papyrus*, which is made by flattening plant stalks. They also wrote on *parchment,* which is goat hide. The writings were rolled up on scrolls and stored in clay jars.

Start by dividing the cardboard circle into sections: Use the ruler and pencil to divide the circle in halves, then quarters, then eighths, and then sixteenths. Squeeze in one more so you have 17 sections, an uneven number. Draw a dot on the edge of the circle on each line. Cut slits about ½ inch long at all 17 dots. Now you've made the loom.

Begin *warping*, or stringing, the loom with yarn. Pull the end of the yarn through a slit and wind the yarn back and forth across the plate, moving in a clockwise direction, slipping it into each slit and bringing it around behind the tabs.

Now you are ready to begin. The yarn you weave into the warp is called the *woof*. Begin weaving with

a piece of yarn about 1 yard long. Wrap it around a Popsicle stick, to work as the *shuttle*. Begin in the center. Weave the yarn in an over-then-under pattern and then repeat, over then under, hiding the end of your yarn behind your work. Keep going over and under, around and around. Add new yarn by tying it to the end of the woof and tucking the knotted ends behind the weaving. When you get to the outside rim, you can knot and clip the yarn and hang it up, leaving the weaving on the loom as a frame. Or, cut the *warp* yarns at the back and tie them together in pairs as you slip the woven mat off the loom's slits.

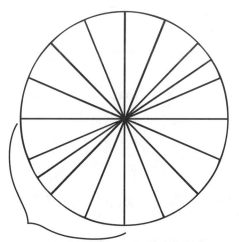

An extra section was put in here to make an uneven number of lines.

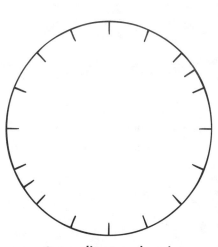

Cut a slit at each point.

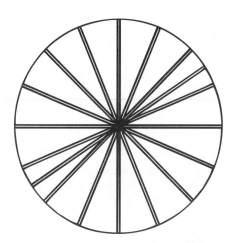

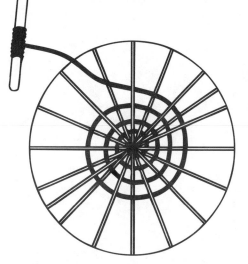

Begin weaving at the center, repeating an over-then-under pattern around and around the circle.

A lot of stories are told about spinners and weavers. In one, a girl named Arachne boasted that she could weave better than Athena, the goddess of weaving. After Athena won the contest she turned the girl into a spider to weave webs forever. The Greek word for spider is *arachne*, from which we get our scientific name for spiders, *arachnids*.

Sappho was a mother and schoolmistress who ran a boarding school for young girls. She wrote beautiful poetry. A few fragments still survive, almost 2,700 years later.

Young girls played a game in which five little stones were thrown in the air and caught on the back of the hand.

STRING ART

Weavers must remember complicated patterns and be sure they repeat them in the right places. Here's a fun activity that uses repeated angles to make an interesting design.

STRING AN ANGLE

This makes a curved design out of straight lines called a *parabolic curve*. Make a simple 8-hole design to see how it works, and then make larger, more complicated curves. You can use any size piece of cardboard and combine angles, circles, squares—any shape you want. Use threads in different colors to get unusual effects.

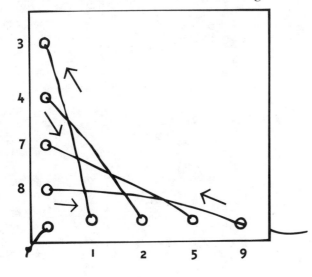

Materials
Lightweight cardboard

Pencil

Ruler

1-2 skeins embroidery floss (or more, depending on your project)

Embroidery needle

Tape

String an angle to make a parabolic curve

Draw two straight lines that meet at one corner in the center of the cardboard. Mark off points every ¼ inch along the two lines. Make the same number of points for both lines. Use embroidery needle to poke a hole at each point.

Thread one end of embroidery thread through the needle. Bring the threaded needle from the back to the front of the plate through a hole at the end of one line. Pull the thread through until only a short piece is left, and tape that to the back. Stitch the holes across from point to point, following the drawing. When you run out of thread, tape the end to the back of the cardboard and begin with new thread in the next hole.

Even though the thread runs in straight lines, it makes a curve. Try changing the angle and the design by making the holes farther apart along one edge and changing the shape of the cardboard from a square to a rectangle. Just be sure to have the same number of holes on each side of the cardboard.

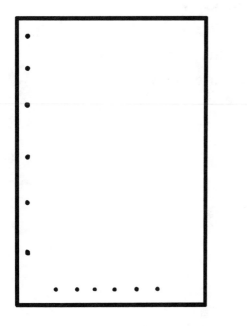

Try putting the holes closer together or farther apart on one side. Be sure both sides have the same number of holes.

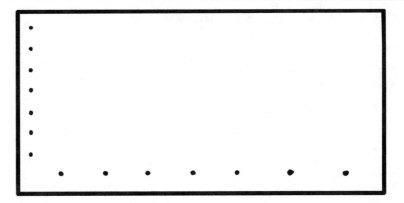

STRING A CIRCLE

(Adult help suggested.)
Cover the plywood with fabric or felt and secure it to the back with glue or staples. Use the paper circle as a pattern. Use the pencil and ruler to mark points around the plate's edge every 1/4 inch. Lay the circle on the plywood and hammer a nail along the edge of the plate at every marked point. Now you're ready to string the circle.

Begin at any point wrapping the string around the first nail and crossing over to the nail directly across from the first. Wrap behind the nail next to the second and come back to the nail next to the first. Keep going around the circle, and an interesting design will emerge. You can change it by using one color thread wrapped on top of another. For another circle, try wrapping across the circle to another point not directly across from your first nail. That will create an open circle in the center of the larger string circle.

Materials

Plywood, 12 by 12 inches or larger

Fabric or felt to cover the plywood

Glue or stapler

Cardboard circle from pizza or heavyweight paper plate

Pencil

Ruler

1 box 1-inch-long, 17-gauge-wire nails

Hammer

Colored string, yarn, or embroidery thread

Wrap the string around the nail directly across, and then around the nail beside this second nail.

Experiment with different colors and putting one circle design on top of another.

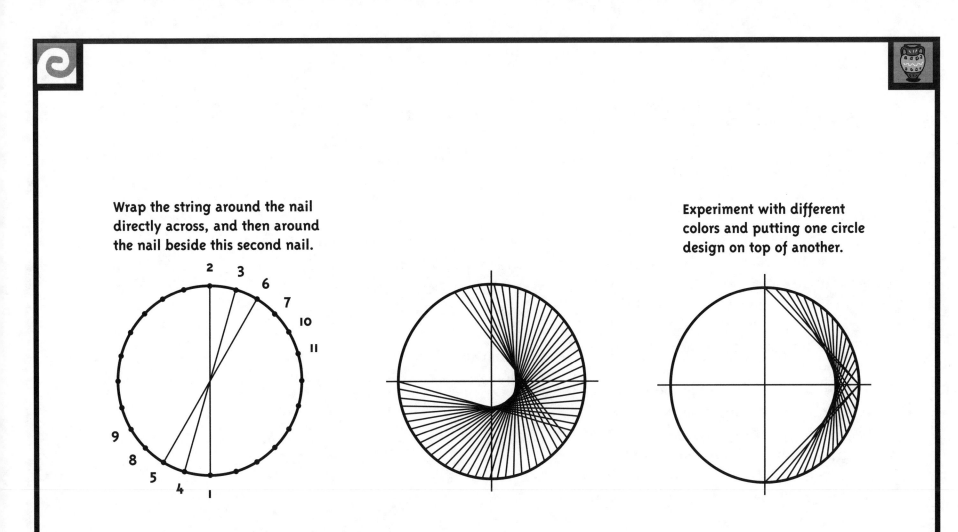

By wrapping the string on a nail that's not opposite from the first wrap, you will make a design that's open in the center.

SEVEN WONDERS OF THE WORLD

There were tourists in ancient Greek times and they wanted to see the sights. The Seven Wonders of the World were the big marvels of the time. Travelers used the list as a guide to sights that should be seen around the Mediterranean region. They were chosen because they were the biggest man-made structures of the time.

Of all the wonders of ancient times, only the Pyramids still exist. Others were destroyed in earthquakes and war. Since the time of ancient Greece, many people have made lists of the greatest wonders of their time. Make a list of today's seven wonders. Use these ideas to help you: canals, buildings, bridges, space vehicles, scientific discoveries, and inventions.

What would you pick as the seven natural wonders? Would you include Mount Saint Helens volcano, the Grand Canyon, Old Faithful, and the Sahara Desert?

1. The Pyramids of Giza in Egypt
2. Hanging Gardens of Babylon
3. Mausoleum of Halicarnassus
4. Temple of Artemis at Ephesus
5. Statue of Zeus at Olympia
6. Pharos at Alexandria, the world's first lighthouse
7. Colossus of Rhodes, a one-hundred-foot-tall statue of the sun god Helios

Seven Wonders of the World

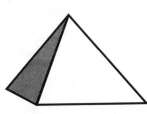

Mausoleum at Halicarnassus

Temple of Artemis at Ephesus

Great Pyramid of Giza

Hanging Garden of Babylon

Statue of Zeus at Olympia

Colossus of Rhodes

Pharos at Alexandria

SIMPLE PULLEY

Workers used *pulleys* to build the huge elaborate buildings and structures in ancient Greece. With a pulley, a heavy weight could be raised in the air by pulling on a rope. Oxen or several men could pull on this rope to lift a large stone slab or column. Wheels that look like enormous hamster exercise wheels were built so that men could walk inside these to help turn pulleys to lift weights, too.

Materials

Wire coat hanger

Ruler

Wire cutters

Empty spool from thread

String

✴ (Adult help suggested.)
Cut the hanger so both ends are about 6 inches long. Bend the ends through the holes in the ends of the thread spool and twist the ends to keep the wires from spreading.

   Hang the pulley from a hook or doorway. Tie one end of the string to an object. Slide the string over the pulley. Watch how as you pull on the string it lifts the weight.

Greek scientists and inventors made a lot of devices that could have been used as labor-saving mechanical and industrial machinery. However, such inventions were never put to use because there were so many slaves and labor was so cheap.

Cut off the bottom of a hanger.

← 6 inches

2 Push the ends through the spool.

3 Bend up the ends and wrap to hold.

Pull down on the string to raise the load.

4

OLYMPIAD

The Greeks enjoyed competing and watching others compete in athletic competition. They held four national festivals, the isthmian, Pythian, Nemean, and Olympian games. The series of games at Olympia was held every four years in the summer. Olympia was a sacred valley dedicated to the worship of Zeus. The Olympic games were started to honor Zeus in 776 B.C.

Greeks came from many different city-states to compete. All contestants were naked and barefoot during competition. Women couldn't compete—they couldn't even watch the games. One woman broke the rules. Her son was a young boxer who had been trained by his father, but when his father died, she took over his training. She dressed like a man so she could watch her son compete in the Olympiad. When he won, she was so excited that she raced to congratulate him and her toga slipped. After that, the trainers had to be naked during the games, too, to prevent any more females from sneaking in.

Centuries later, Greece became part of the Roman Empire. When the Olympic games were held during Roman rule, women were allowed to watch and participate. By then, nakedness was no longer required.

The foot race was the most important competition. They also had the pentathlon, which included the long jump, sprinting, the discus throw, the javelin throw, and wrestling. Boxing, horse racing, and other events were included. Teenage boys competed in three events: the two-hundred-meter race, wrestling, and boxing.

There were musical events in the early Olympiad. Winners of musical contests won silver money and gold decorations. For winners in physical fitness and beauty contests, a shield was given. (Remember, only men could participate.) For winners in gymnastics and horse racing the prize was an urn of oil from the sacred olive trees. Sometimes winners received crowns of wild olive branches and had poems written about them, and they lived the rest of their lives supported by the government because they were considered heroes.

In A.D. 394, the Romans had control of Greece, and the emperor Theodosius banned the games.

They weren't revived again until 1896.

Why not put together a series of games for your family or neighborhood? Think up some challenging and fun events like these.

Ring Wrestling: Use wooden or plastic rings. Two players each try to pull the ring out of the other's hand.

Potato Put: Compete to see who can hurl a potato the farthest.

Wheelbarrow Race: On each team of two partners, one uses his or her arms to crawl, while the other holds up the crawler's feet. Race against others to the finish line.

Water Cup Relay: Teams compete to see who can run across the track with cups of water. Whichever team fills its coffee can first wins. Use a ruler to measure the water level.

Straw Blowing: Competitors stand on a starting line, put drinking straws between their lips, and then blow them as far as they can.

Clothes Exchange Relay: Teams compete to see who can put large shirts, jeans, and hats on over their clothing, race to the other line, take them off, and then tag the next relay player to go put them on and return.

Whistling Crackers: Players are each given a soda cracker. Each player must eat it and whistle as quickly as he or she can. The first or the loudest whistler wins.

Bubble Gum Race: Players are all given wrapped bubble gum. The first one to blow a big bubble wins, first to burst a big bubble wins, first to get it all over his or her face wins, and so forth!

Go ahead and think up some more fun games. For everyone, a lot of lemonade and Popsicles make it fun. And you don't have to wait four years to try it all again!

THE BEGINNING OF THE END

The Greek city-states were nearly always warring with each other or armies from other areas. Wars ravaged the countryside and the peasants were starving. They sold out their small farms and moved to the cities. That only made things worse. In 330 B.C. the Macedonian army invaded and defeated the Greek city-states. Their leader, a young man known as Alexander the Great, became the ruler of Greece.

THE AGE OF ROME

After Alexander the Great died in 323 B.C., the Greek Empire began to weaken. At the same time, another group of people, the Romans, in a neighboring country that's now Italy, began to build an empire of their own. The Romans started as a small community of sheepherders in central Italy and became one of the most powerful civilizations in the world. In 146 B.C., Roman armies defeated the Macedonians and took over Greece, as well as nearly all the other countries in the area. The Roman Empire grew to rule fifty to seventy million people, spread out over almost half of Europe, most of the Middle East, and the north coast of Africa. The Romans adopted many Greek ideas about things like art, clothing, foods, architecture, religion, and math. There are three periods in the history of the ancient Romans:

1. The kingdom (753–509 B.C.), a time when kings and their royal families ruled. The people had no choice.
2. The republic (509–31 B.C.), a time when citizens voted for government representatives to run the country.
3. The empire (31 B.C.–A.D. 476), when power was taken from the people by dictators, called *emperors*, who ran the government.

At first there were kings who ran the government and controlled the kingdom. Then people grew angry at having no choice so they threw out the last king and began voting for their own leaders.

During the time of the republic, people were able to vote for government officials of their choice. Two *consuls* were elected to run the government. They had to agree on what should be done. They were elected every year.

A group of wealthy men was elected to the *senate* by all freemen (no women or slaves could cast ballots). The senate gave advice to the consuls. They were in the senate for life.

All the men in the senate were from wealthy families called *patrician*s; ordinary working citizens, most of whom were poor, were called *plebeians*. There was a continual struggle between the many poor citizens and the few wealthy families who held all the power.

In times of trouble or war, the senate could elect a dictator who had absolute power. Some dictators were popular with the people (like Julius Caesar), but when they declared themselves emperors, the people had no choice but to blindly follow their leadership and laws.

MAP OF ANCIENT ROME

The Roman Empire at its peak, about A.D. 120.

DRESS UP ROMAN

TOGA

The *toga* looks a lot like the Greek chiton, but Roman clothes were longer and fuller than the Greeks', using many more yards of cloth. Fabrics were wool and linen, woven heavier and thicker for winter wear. The toga took careful wrapping and tucking. Helping the master or mistress drape the toga correctly was sometimes the job of special slaves.

The toga was $2\frac{1}{2}$ times as long as a person's height, and the width was two times his or her height. People wore a *tunica*, which was sort of a long undershirt, under the toga or when hanging around the house. When the weather was cold, people wore up to four tunicas under the toga.

Folds were so important that the wearer tried not to move around too much. Slaves carefully arranged the folds. The night before wearing, slaves would put small pieces of wood in the fabric to form the folds. Small bits of lead were sewn along the edges of the toga to weight the fabric, making it drape into better folds.

The toga was too clumsy to work in, so when you saw someone on the street wearing it you knew he was wealthy and had no need to labor. The law said that only freemen could wear togas. Slaves wore *loincloths*, or cloth wrapped like a diaper and tied around their waists. Workmen wore loincloths, too, and sometimes short capes. Boys wore togas with purple trimming on the edges until they became sixteen years old. Then they were considered men and changed to solid white togas. Girls wore togas with purple trim until they married and then they no longer used the purple trim. Soldiers wore togas in battle, but then they tied the end around their waists instead of tossing it over their left shoulders.

Before you begin, find an old bedsheet and be certain to ask an adult if it's OK to cut it. Then measure your height against a wall and mark it with a pencil. Multiply this number by 2.5 to figure out the size toga you'll need to make it authentic.

Materials

White bedsheet, cut to 2½ times your height (ask for permission before cutting)

Tape measure

Pencil

Scissors

Togas were shaped like this. Fold it in half before draping.

1. Fold it lengthwise. Throw one end over the left shoulder, leaving about one-third of it hanging in front.

2. Wrap the rest across the back and bring it under the right arm and up over the left shoulder again.

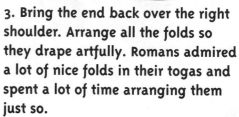

3. Bring the end back over the right shoulder. Arrange all the folds so they drape artfully. Romans admired a lot of nice folds in their togas and spent a lot of time arranging them just so.

STOLA

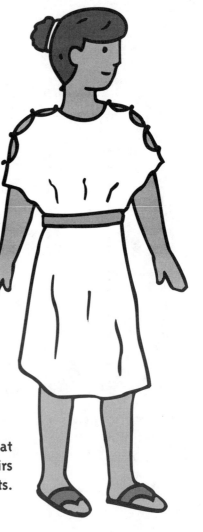

Roman women wore a *stola*, which was like the Greek chiton but didn't have as much draping material. Sometimes they wore a robe over it, called a *palla*. A stola was an ankle-length tunic. With a ribbon belt tied at the waist, the stola was pulled out above the waist so it folded down over the belt. Girls wore stolas that reached to just above the knee, without a belt. Some stolas fastened with buttons down the shoulders and arms. If a stola was long, it dragged behind like a train. Some were made very wide so they hung in pleats at the bottom. Stolas were trimmed with blue, red, yellow, or gold bands or fringe. Stolas were simple in Rome's early years, but later they were made in bright colors or even made of see-through silk.

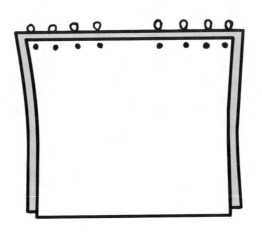

Make a stola from 2 pieces of fabric. Fasten over the shoulders with buttons or pins.

Stolas worn by women were belted at the waist. Girls wore theirs without belts.

PALLA

Pallas were made of bright-colored wool decorated with embroidery. Some fastened at the shoulders with fancy pins. Women added shoulder capes, scarves, or handkerchiefs as accessories.

**Pallas were worn like shawls or capes.
They were large squares of cloth.**

The Romans hadn't discovered how to make soap, so how did they wash their clothes? They took them to special workmen, called *fullers*, who specialized in cleaning clothing. Fullers used several washtubs made of brick. In the first tub of water, a fuller stomped barefoot on clothes to loosen the soil. Next, workmen pulled the clothes out of the water and rubbed any stains that were still on the clothes. Then they were rinsed in a tub of fresh water. The rinse was important, because fullers used clay and urine to get the clothing clean. After rinsing, the clothing was hung on wood poles and brushed with *teasels* to fluff up the fabric. Last, they were draped over wooden frames to dry.

MAKEUP

Roman women wore a lot of makeup. They painted their faces with a white paint and rubbed red or purple paint on their lips and cheeks. They used black eye shadow made from wood ashes or gold eye shadow made of saffron. (Saffron is made from dried flowers and is used in cooking today.) They rubbed sheep's fat on their fingernails to make them look shiny. They used blue paint to outline veins in the face, neck, arms, and legs. They used lemon juice to bleach out freckles, and they whitened their teeth by rubbing them with a pumice stone.

When the Roman army captured German slaves and brought them back to Rome, everyone was wild about their blonde hair. Women bleached their hair blonde using saffron, and they dusted their hair with silver dust, or if they were wealthy, powdered it with pure gold. Blonde wigs were made from slaves' hair and were very popular.

It was against the law for Roman citizens to wear trousers around Rome, but it was OK if foreigners wore them. If men's legs got cold, they wrapped fabric bands around them, like large bandages.

Women also wore veils, fastening them at the back of their head and letting them hang down the back and shoulders. Brides wore bright orange veils, the color of flames, to their wedding. Girls tied their hair up with ribbons, strings of pearls, and jewels. Wreaths of leaves and flowers were popular for everyone who could afford to buy them or who was clever enough to make them. Women sometimes wore hair nets made of gold or silver thread. Women and girls tied kerchiefs around their hair at night so their fancy hairdos wouldn't get mussed while sleeping.

Romans (men and women) liked rows of curls in their hair, and special hairdresser slaves used curling irons and hair oils to help the curls hold their shape. Men and women both wore hairpieces to make their own hair look thicker. Men who were bald sometimes painted on hair so they looked like they had a short haircut—from a distance! Romans loved fancy hairdos so much that there were even statues made with changeable hairdos. The top of the head was removable so pieces with different hairstyles could be used.

MAKE SANDALS

B y law, boots had to be worn with a toga. Most people went bare-foot (at least in the house) or wore sandals or shoes that fastened with straps tied around the foot, ankle, or lower leg. Soldiers in the army wore sandals with nail heads stuck in the sole, called *hob-nailed* soles. The shoes didn't wear out as fast, even with all the walking they did. (The Roman army walked nearly everywhere they went; only the elite equestrians rode horseback.) Imagine the noise along a cobble-stone roadway when a legion of soldiers marched past!

Materials

Paper bag

Pencil

Scissors

1 chamois (available at automotive supply stores) or 2 9- by 12-inch pieces of felt

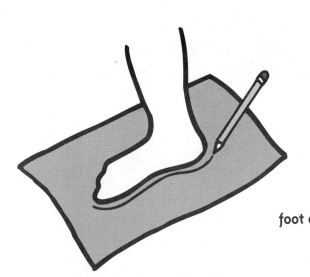

Trace your foot to make a pattern.

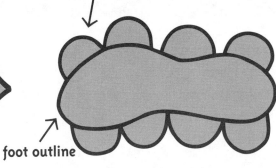

Draw 4 half circles on each side.

foot outline

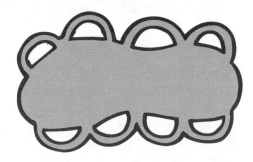

Cut 2 sandals from the chamois. Trim out the inside of the half circles.

Cut laces from circles of chamois.

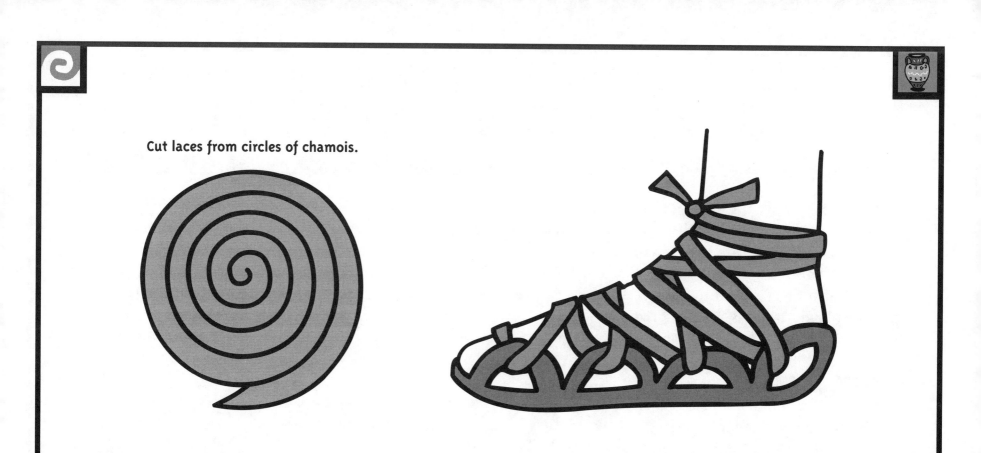

Use the paper bag to make a pattern from your foot. Stand on the paper and trace around your foot. Make 4 half-circle shapes along both sides of the foot. Cut out the pattern. Lay it on the chamois and trace around it. Cut out. Reverse the pattern and trace and cut a sandal for the other foot.

Cut out the centers of the half-circle shapes, leaving about ½ inch all around.

From the scraps of chamois, make the laces. That's easy if you use a large circle shape of chamois. Cut along the outer edge, making a strip ½ inch wide. Keep cutting round and round into the center. Gently stretch the strip to straighten it. Make as many pieces of lacing as you need. You can knot the ends to connect them.

To put on the sandal, slide the lacing through the openings, crisscrossing the laces across your foot as you go. Tie the laces around your ankle. If you have plenty of lacing, go ahead and lace up to your knee, like the Romans did.

BEADED BRACELET

Girls and women who could afford it wore necklaces and chains of gold with jewels and pearls. Some chains had gold charms in the form of scissors, keys, anchors, saws, hammers, or other tools.

One popular bracelet looked like a snake wrapped around the arm. Ribbons were also tied around the upper and lower arms. Men wore massive arm rings (bracelets) that they won as prizes in contests.

Make a clever beaded bracelet for yourself.

Materials

Up to 50 tiny gold safety pins

About 118 small beads (be sure the holes are big enough to put the safety pins through)

Open each pin, thread 3 beads on it, and close it. Lay the pins on the table in rows of 3. Thread the beaded pins on joining pins, going through the tails of the first row and the heads of the next row. Put the beaded pins on the joining pin in a pattern: tail, head, tail, head, tail, head. Use another joining pin to connect the next row of beaded pins the same way. Keep adding beaded pins until the bracelet is the size you want. A joining pin will be the clasp.

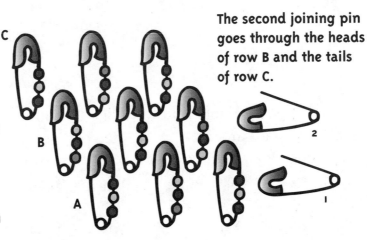

The second joining pin goes through the heads of row B and the tails of row C.

The first joining pin goes through the heads of row A and the tails of row B.

Keep going! Add rows of pins and joining pins.

EARRINGS

Roman women wore earrings that hung on their ears from loops of gold thread. Pearls or jewels were strung on the threads so they dangled below the ear.

Materials

Gold thread, narrow ribbon, or yarn

Scissors

Buttons, beads, or tinted salad macaroni for jewels

✳ Cut a piece of yarn about 6 inches long. String 2 or 3 jewels on it. Tie the ends in a knot and loop the earring over your ear.

String some jewels.

Hang the loops from your ears.

DISAPPEARING EGGSHELL

Romans loved to wear pearls. The whiter and bigger they were, the more they were willing to pay for them. Cleopatra, the Queen of Egypt, showed off for everyone at one Roman banquet where she was a guest. She drank a pearl! Actually she dropped a pearl worth 10 million *sestertia* (Roman dollars) into a glass of vinegar. The guests watched it dissolve in the vinegar, and then Cleopatra drank it.

Try this experiment for yourself. Don't use a pearl, though!

Materials

Shell from 1 egg, empty
Drinking glass or jar
1 cup vinegar

✴ Place the eggshell in the bottom of the glass and pour in vinegar to cover. Let it sit overnight. By morning, the eggshell will have disappeared. Like Cleopatra's pearl, the acid in the vinegar dissolved it!

vinegar

Tomorrow the eggshell will be gone!

Romans wore false teeth carved from elephant tusk ivory. They held these fake teeth in place with gold thread tied to good teeth.

BATH TIME!

Romans enjoyed bathing every day in huge indoor bathhouses built just for bathing. The baths were the most popular places in Roman towns. Bathhouses included gardens, museums, libraries, massage rooms, gyms, steam rooms, and sunning parlors where people worked on their tans. Stoves heated pipes that warmed the water for the warm and hot baths. Warm pipes under the floors heated the bathhouse in winter. One Roman bathhouse could hold thirty-two thousand people in both hot- and cold-water swimming pools.

Women and girls bathed before noon; the rest of the time was for men. Bathhouses were open at night, too, lit with oil lamps in the walls.

BATH OIL

Romans didn't have bath soap. They rubbed scented oil on their skin (or had a slave do it) and then scraped the oil off with a curved tool called a *strigil*.

Enjoy taking a bath as much as the Romans did with this easy recipe for bath oil.

Pour some of your bath oil into the running water as the tub fills.

safflower
oil

shampoo

glycerine

Materials
2 tablespoons safflower oil
1 tablespoon glycerin (sold in drugstores)
1 tablespoon shampoo
Measuring spoons
Baby food jar or small jar with lid

⭐ Put the safflower oil, glycerin, and shampoo in the jar, secure the lid, and shake to mix. Shake again just before using in the bathtub. Pour some of the bath oil into the stream of hot running water as the tub fills.

Make several jars of oil for gifts. Cover the lid with paint, markers, or a pretty scrap of cloth. Tie ribbon or bright yarn around the jar, and it's ready to be given to someone special.

Romans began work at dawn but worked only seven hours in summer and less than six in winter. The court officials and judges worked long hours because the courts were open to hear cases that went on as long as people wanted to present them. Most slaves and workmen had afternoons off and headed to the public baths. The Romans had about one holiday for every working day.

DINNER ROMAN STYLE

Early in the morning Romans usually just had a drink of water. They ate a late breakfast or early lunch of bread dipped in wine, an egg, and maybe some olives and figs. The biggest meal of the day was in late afternoon.

Romans ate while lying on their side on a couch, where they couldn't work knives and forks very well, so they ate with their fingers or used a spoon. If people ate at someone else's house, they took their own spoon with them. Customers at taverns and inns ate while sitting at benches. Most foods were made of grains, vegetables, and eggs. Fish and goose were also popular. No one drank milk; instead they mixed wine with water for a beverage. Snow was carried down from the mountains on donkey packs and stored underground. It was used to cool drinks.

In ancient Rome, families didn't gather together for meals. There was no kitchen table to sit around, either. Children were raised by baby-sitters or nannies. Boys had a pedagogue, a teacher who was their companion and slave. For most meals, children ate with the nanny or pedagogue. If they ate with their parents, the father reclined on a couch, the mother sat at his feet, and the children sat on the floor.

Families weren't large; three children was the ideal, but many couples didn't have that many. Adoption was very common. People even adopted adults if they had no children. That way they could leave their fortune to someone they had chosen.

Romans were never alone. If they were poor, they lived with their whole family crowded in one room. If they were wealthy, slaves dressed them, put on their shoes, even slept on the floor of their master or mistresses's bedroom or in the doorway to act as a guard. Banquets were something everyone looked forward to in ancient Rome, at least for people important or wealthy enough to get an invitation to one. The correct number of guests for a dinner party was nine. There's a good reason for keeping the number at nine. The diners lay on three couches set up in a U shape around a small table. If more than nine guests were invited, other tables and couches were set up, in groups of nine. The diners reclined while they ate propped on their left arms; they stretched for food and drink with their right hands. Forks were unknown, and knives and spoons rarely used. Most people ate with their fingers, although they did use fingerbowls and napkins spread over the edge of the couch to keep it clean. Guests brought their own napkin and used it to carry home leftovers they hadn't had time to eat. It's hard to believe they ran out of time, since banquets were long—some lasted ten hours. Between courses the guests watched acrobats, clowns, or dancers; heard a concert; told riddles; held a lottery; or just enjoyed conversation.

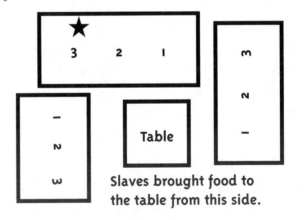

Slaves brought food to the table from this side.

Here's how a Roman dinner party was set up. Three guests lay on each couch. The center table held the food. The honored spot was where the star is. The most important diner was given that place.

Roman water pipes, cooking pots, and cups were made of lead. Historians think the Roman people were poisoned by the lead. Lead makes people lose their appetite and their ability to taste foods. Maybe that's why they didn't have a lot of food choices.

Everyone got their water at public fountains in the streets or bought it from people who delivered it at the door. Most people lived in large apartment buildings that didn't have bathrooms. They had to pay to use public toilets or use *latrines* (ditches) for free. The public toilets were nicely decorated, and the toilets were all in a room where people could visit. The ancient Romans weren't shy about such things.

Most poor Romans had no way to cook their own food. Apartment buildings were several stories tall and made of wood. Fires were always burning them down. Renters were discouraged from cooking or heating in the buildings, and the cost of charcoal was too much for many. Instead, people ate in taverns or bars or took food to the bakers, where they had it cooked for them in the oven. Take-out shops, called *thermopolia*, were especially popular. These places served snacks that were kept hot in containers sunk into the counters, just like today's cafeterias.

Romans had their slaves raise birds in cages. The birds were fed grass seeds, crushed figs, and wheat flour. Milk was given to fatten snails and caged mice were given nuts. The average person didn't even eat that well!

Childhood didn't last long in Rome. Boys went to school to the age of twelve, after which only the wealthy boys continued. Sons of citizens could join the army as early as sixteen. Many girls got married at twelve, and at fourteen they were considered adults. At the age of seventeen, one boy who had been in the army was in charge of the Roman police, supervised executions, and governed the minting of coins. At sixteen years old another boy was already a colonel in the army and had presented his first law cases at court.

ARTICHOKES

Really a thistle, the artichoke was very popular in ancient Rome. The Greeks had eaten them, too. Artichokes grew wild in the area around the Mediterranean Sea. Today, people in Rome, Italy, really like artichokes—each person there eats about 175 per year! In the United States, most artichokes are grown near Castroville, California, where they hold an annual artichoke festival. Artichokes ripen for harvest from September to May. Look for them in the produce section of the grocery store.

Here's how you cook 'chokes.

Ingredients

4 servings

4 medium-sized artichokes (you'll need 1 artichoke per person)

6 quarts water

¼ cup salad oil

2 tablespoons lemon juice

1 teaspoon salt

1 cup mayonnaise

Utensils

Kitchen scissors (if desired)

Serrated plastic knife

Large pot

Measuring spoons

2 large spoons or tongs

Roman dinner guests bought wreaths and perfumed oils from shops on their way to a dinner party to wear or to give to the host.

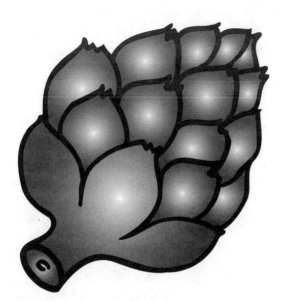

mayonnaise

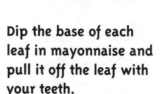

Dip the base of each leaf in mayonnaise and pull it off the leaf with your teeth.

★ (Adult help suggested.)

Pull off the tough small leaves around the stem of each artichoke and use the serrated plastic knife to trim the stem. If you like, you can use kitchen scissors to snip across the tip of each leaf to remove the sharp points at the end of each leaf. Rinse the artichokes in cool water.

Put the water in a large pot. Add salad oil, lemon juice, and salt to the water. Add the artichokes and heat the water to boiling. Turn the heat to low and simmer for 40 minutes. There's no need to put a lid on the pot.

Use two large spoons or tongs to remove each artichoke from the water.

That's all there is to it! To enjoy your artichokes, pluck the leaves off one at a time, and dip the "meaty" inner part of the leaf into mayonnaise. Turn the leaf meaty side down and put it in your mouth, scraping the meat off with your teeth as you pull the leaf back out of your mouth. Throw the leaf away.

After you've enjoyed the meaty leaves, you'll come to the inside of the artichoke, which is a fuzzy core surrounding the *heart*. Use the knife to cut off the fuzzy core covering the heart and throw this away. Pull or cut out the heart, and cut this prize section into bite-sized pieces, and dip it into the mayonnaise before eating. Yum!

BEAN SALAD

Romans ate a lot of fresh vegetables, and salads were a favorite food. Here's one quite a bit like the dishes eaten in ancient Rome. You can store it in the refrigerator for one day.

(Note: You can substitute ½ cup Italian salad dressing for the oil and vinegar.)

Romans used dry beans to cast their votes in some elections.

Ingredients

2 15½ ounce cans garbanzo beans (sometimes called chickpeas)

2 green onions

1 tomato, chopped

2 tablespoons salad oil

2 tablespoons red wine vinegar

½ cup fresh chopped parsley or 2 tablespoons dried parsley

2 tablespoons fresh chopped chives or 1 tablespoon dried chives

Salt and pepper to taste

Utensils

Colander

Large bowl

Measuring spoons

Spoon

8 servings

 Drain the garbanzo beans and rinse them in the colander. Mix all the ingredients together in the large bowl. Chill in the refrigerator until it's time to eat.

garbanzo beans (chickpeas)

dressing

CRUSTULUM

12 servings

We know what the Romans called *crustulum* as garlic toast, but here we're making it the way they did in ancient Rome. What English word do you think came from the Latin word *crustulum*? (Hint: It's around the edges of bread.)

Ingredients

loaf Italian or French bread, sliced
1 garlic clove
½ cup olive oil

Utensils

Serrated plastic knife
Toaster
Pastry brush

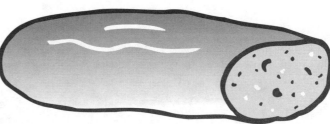

olive oil

✴ Toast the bread slices. Trim and peel the garlic clove. Rub the garlic all over the toast. Brush olive oil on the bread. That's it!

The word *salary* comes from *salaria*, which is Latin for "salt", and dates from the Roman practice of paying soldiers in salt as part of their pay.

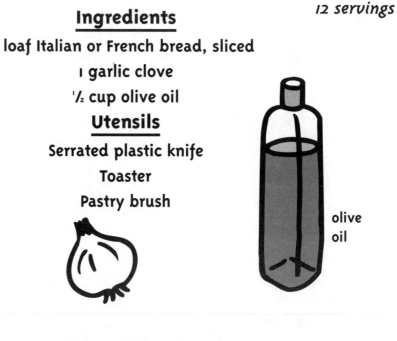

OLIVE ROLLS

Ingredients

12 rolls

1 loaf frozen bread dough

1 15-ounce can Manzanilla olives (the green ones with pimento stuffing)

1 egg and 1 tablespoon of water, stirred together

Garlic powder (if desired)

Parmesan cheese

Utensils

Baking pan, greased

Pastry brush

(Adult help suggested.)

Let the dough thaw out for a few hours. Drain the olives. Before you begin to make the rolls, preheat the oven to 350° F.

Pull off clumps of dough about the size of an egg. Push an olive or two into the center and pinch the dough around it to seal the olive inside. Place the rolls pinched side down on the greased baking pan.

Use the pastry brush to paint the rolls with the egg and water mixture. Then sprinkle a little garlic powder and Parmesan cheese on top if you like.

Allow the rolls to rise until double in size. Bake until golden brown, about 15 minutes. Let them cool and then enjoy! It's fun and tasty to find hidden olives in the warm rolls.

The Romans washed their dishes by rubbing them with fine sand and then rinsing. They didn't have soap. Soap was probably invented by the Tartars and was unknown in Europe until A.D. 700.

CINNAMON RAISIN ROLLS

Wealthy people had a bakery built onto their houses; everyone else bought baked breads from shops or street vendors. Rolls were popular because they were made of Romans' favorite food: bread. Plus, they could be eaten quickly and easily. Spices and dried fruits made them even tastier. Use cinnamon and raisins to flavor bread dough—creating a tasty treat that's only a couple thousand years old.

Cinnamon bark was brought to Rome by ship from Indonesia. It was transported in outrigger canoes 4,500 miles, and then went by ship up the coast of East Africa to the Red Sea. The Arabs brought the cinnamon to the Romans and made up magic myths about where and how they got it. They didn't want the Romans finding out because then the Arabs would be out of business.

Ingredients

10 to 12 rolls

Flour to dust work surface

1 loaf frozen bread dough, thawed

½ to 1 stick margarine
(let it sit out a bit to soften)

½ cup packed brown sugar

2 teaspoons cinnamon

¼ cup raisins

Utensils

Rolling pin

1 12-inch-long piece of
string or sewing thread

Greased cookie sheet

Paper towels

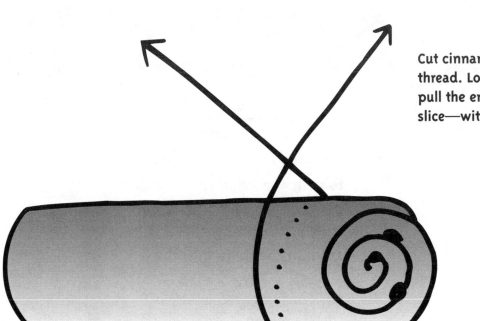

Cut cinnamon roll dough with a piece of sewing thread. Loop it around the roll of dough and pull the ends in opposite directions. A perfect slice—without a knife!

(Adult help suggested.)
Preheat oven to 400° F.

Dust the work surface with a bit of flour so the dough won't stick. Roll out the dough to make a rectangle about ¼ inch thick. Spread softened margarine on it. Sprinkle on the brown sugar, then the cinnamon, and then the raisins. Begin rolling up the dough at one long end to make a long log. Cut the dough into slices about 1 inch wide. An easy way is

with a piece of thread. Hold both ends in your hands, slip the thread around the roll of dough, and pull the threads together. The thread slices right through the soft dough without a mess and with no knife to wash! Place the rolls on the greased cookie sheet. Brush the tops with softened margarine. Cover with paper towels and let rise in a warm place for about 20 minutes. Bake for 20 minutes.

BREAD IN A BAG

It was said at the time that the only things Romans cared about were bread and circuses. Bread was given away free. Roman citizens were given free grain to make their own bread with if they were poor (one out of three Roman citizens was poor). Eventually every citizen received free grain. As different leaders were elected they gave away more food, adding oil, baked bread (instead of grain), pork fat, and even wine. The citizens were happy to vote for leaders who would give them more free food.

Supplying this much grain became a challenge. It took so much grain that one-third of it had to come from Egypt by boat. The Roman army had to conquer new lands in order to get enough land to grow all the wheat that the Roman citizens needed. Ships were constantly being built to bring the grain to Rome as quickly as possible. The city went into a panic when the ships failed to arrive on time.

What kinds of bread did ancient Romans eat? Some kinds are in bakeries today, such as baguettes, croissants, crumpets, suet bread, cheese bread, pancakes, and wafers. Plain bread was torn in chunks and dipped in wine or goat's milk for a snack. Here's a fun way to make bread. Too bad Roman bakers didn't have plastic bags to save them a mess.

Ingredients
20-24 servings

3 cups flour plus extra to dust the work surface

1 package fast-rising yeast

2 teaspoons sugar

1 cup warm water

1 teaspoon salt

1 tablespoon vegetable oil

Utensils

Measuring cup

Large plastic bag, with twist tie

Measuring spoons

Rolling pin

2 loaf pans, greased

Baking rack

> Romans were the first people to eat hen's eggs often. Before that, people raised birds only for fighting. The Romans learned how to incubate eggs from the Greeks.

Knead the dough in the bag to mix the ingredients.

![star] (Adult help suggested.)
Preheat oven to 400° F.

In the large plastic bag, combine 1 cup flour, and the yeast, sugar, and warm water. Close the bag with the twist tie. Knead and work the bag with your fingers to mix everything together. When the dough is completely mixed, let it sit and rest for 10 minutes. (This time allows the yeast to create air bubbles, which will make the bread rise light and fluffy.)

Open the bag and add 1 cup of flour, the salt, and vegetable oil. Close the bag with the twist tie and work the dough until the flour is all mixed in. Slowly add the final cup of flour. Open the bag and add a little bit at a time, mixing thoroughly. Stop when the dough pulls away from the sides of the bag.

Dust the work surface with flour. Take the dough out of the bag and put it on the work surface. Divide the dough in half. Knead ½ of the dough for 5 minutes, until it's smooth and elastic. If it's too sticky, add a very small amount of flour. Roll the dough into a rectangle. Starting at the small end, roll the dough up into a loaf. Pinch the ends together and turn them under. Place the loaf seam-sid-down in a greased loaf pan, and then let it rise for 30 minutes. Do the same with the other half of the dough.

Bake for 25 minutes.

Remove the pan from the oven. Take the bread from the pan while it's still warm and cool it on the baking rack.

Idaho Wheat Commission

ROMAN ARMY

The Romans needed a huge army to conquer all the lands they wanted to rule. Only men between the ages of seventeen and forty-six who were citizens and owned property could be in the Roman army. At first they were only part-time soldiers; in later centuries many were in the army for twenty years. The soldiers called *legionaries* were organized in groups called *legions*. Legions ranged in size from three thousand to six thousand soldiers. Smaller groups of one hundred were led by a *centurion*. When moving, the army stopped every night, but first they built a camp surrounded by a wooden fence and mounds of earth. A legion's camp had about five hundred tents. There were ten legionaries in each tent. Centurions and important people had their own tents.

MAKE A STANDARD

Have you ever heard someone talk about *upholding* or *maintaining their standards*? Well, that's exactly what Roman armies did.

A soldier called a *signifier* carried his legion's standard, or *signum*, while marching and in battle. The first signums were a bundle of hay tied on top of a pole. Through the years they were made fancier, using gold, silver, ribbons, and cloth flags. In the later years of the Roman Empire, most standards had a gold or silver eagle on top. Below the eagle were various disks, plates, animals, or images of emperors.

The standard was respected by soldiers just as our flag is today. No one would let it fall into enemy hands. If the standard was lost in battle, the entire legion was shamed.

← gold wreath

← ribbon streamers

← paper plates covered with aluminum foil

← yarn fringe

Materials
Small paper plates
Aluminum foil
Scissors
Construction paper
Long cardboard tube
(from a roll of wrapping paper)
Glue gun
Ribbons or strips of cloth
Yarn

A *signifier* was the soldier who carried the group's *signum* or standard.

Make the paper plates look silver by wrapping them with aluminum foil. Cut construction paper into shapes like a wreath, an eagle with wings spread out, or some other symbol you like. Glue the symbols and plates to the paper tube. Add ribbon streamers or strips of cloth. Make yarn fringe by holding one end of the yarn and wrapping it around your hand several times. Pull the yarn off your hand and take the end of the yarn, loop it through the rings of yarn, tie it around the bottom of the paper tube, and knot. Add dabs of glue all the way around the tube to hold the yarn in place.

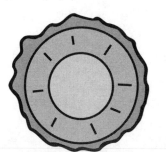

Romans used the first military medals as rewards for bravery. Small round pieces of silver were made to look like the legion's standard. The silver medals were hung on a ribbon of cloth from the soldier's neck or pinned to his toga. One brave soldier fought in 120 battles and received 342 awards.

PAPIER-MÂCHÉ ROMAN ARMY HELMET

★ Blow up the balloon and knot the end. Tear the newspaper into strips about 2 by 3 inches in size. Mix the flour and water in the pie pan or shallow bowl, stirring and adding water until it's like thin pancake batter. Dip each strip of newspaper into the papier-mâché, pull it through your fingers to take off the excess paste, and press it gently onto the balloon. Cover the top half of the balloon with strips, layering the edges of the strips on top of each other. When you've covered the top half of the balloon, place it in an empty coffee can for support until it's dry. Let it dry overnight. Pop the balloon and gently pull it away from the dry helmet base.

Roll a piece of newspaper into a long thin tube and tape to the front to make the visor. Cut out a crest from cardboard for the top of the helmet.

Cut a paper plate to shape to make the back neck piece of the helmet. Tape the neck piece and crest in place with masking tape. Cut out 2 earflap shapes from lightweight cardboard. To attach the earflaps, tape a piece of cloth to the inside of the helmet and to the inside of the flap. It will become a flexible "hinge" so the earflaps will move when you put the helmet on and off. Cover the helmet with at least two more layers of papier-mâché strips pasted on top of each other. Be sure plenty of strips hold the neck piece and crest onto the helmet. Cover the fabric pieces inside the helmet and earflaps with pasted newspaper strips, but leave the fabric hinge uncoated so it will be flexible. Let it dry completely. Finally, paint your helmet gold, silver, or any color you want.

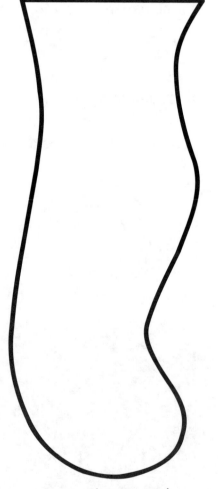

earflap (actual size)

Materials

Large round balloon
Newspaper
1 cup flour
About 2 cups water
Pie pan or shallow bowl
Spoon
Empty coffee can or bowl

Masking tape
Lightweight cardboard
Scissors
Paper plate
2 scraps of cloth,
each about 3 by 3 inches
Gold or silver paint

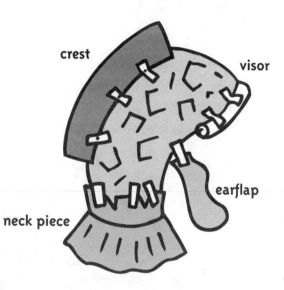

crest

visor

earflap

neck piece

Tape the visor, crest, neck piece, and earflaps to the helmet and cover with layers of pasted newspaper strips.

Paint when completely dry.

Sick people were cared for at home, but for soldiers in the army that wasn't possible. The Roman army took along Greek doctors and set up the first hospitals at military outposts.

While on the march, each soldier carried a pack that weighed between sixty and ninety pounds. It held a saw, chain, rope, tools for digging and building roads, pots and pans to cook in, food, and a leather shield for fighting. Marius devised the *Marian mule*, for soldiers. It made it easier to carry their packs. It was a pole with forked ends with a piece of wood tied across it. Everything was rolled into a bundle and tied to the cross pole.

Roman soldiers didn't spend all their time in battle; they built roads and forts in the conquered territory. Some roads they built are still used today.

MAKE A CATAPULT

Roman legions took catapults into battle. A *catapult* was mainly a large wood beam with a sling hanging from it. Soldiers loaded a large stone into the sling. When the catapult was released the stone was flung into the air. It was easy to smash holes in a fort's wall with a catapult, and it kept soldiers back out of the line of fire of melted lead, pots of fire, pitch torches, burning arrows, and stones that enemies often threw over the fort walls during battle.

Materials

Empty milk carton or shoebox
Plastic spoon
Masking tape
Marshmallows

✴ Tape the spoon handle to the top of the box, letting the bowl of the spoon extend out beyond the edge of the box. To launch marshmallows, simply put one in the spoon, pull it back, and let it fly!

Tape a plastic spoon to a box.

Pull the spoon down to launch a marshmallow upward.

SLINGSHOT

A slingshot is a catapult on a small scale. It's easy to make one.

Materials

Newspaper

Y-shaped tree branch

Thick rubber band

Ball up a few sheets of newspaper to use as weapons. Slide the rubber band down over both sides of the fork in the branch. Grab a newspaper ball and hold it in the middle of the band. Pull the band back and then let go. Watch as the ball flies through the air! Try hitting a target—it's not as easy as it seems.

Slingshot

Pulling back on the band launches the ball in the opposite direction.

The Roman army couldn't be stopped. For battle they built ten-story-high wooden walking towers. The towers had stairs up the inside and a drawbridge at the top that could be let down. They rolled the tower up next to a castle wall, let down the bridge, and hurried over the wall. To cross rivers, they lined up pontoons that each man carried, anchored them in the water with baskets of stones, and laid boards across the top. Then the army just walked across the river. They took up the bridge pieces and carried everything along to the next river.

PAPIER-MÂCHÉ ELEPHANT

Hannibal was twenty-five years old when he took command of the Carthaginian army in Spain. Roman troops had tried to defeat him but couldn't. He surprised them by marching his army across the high mountains in northern Italy called the Alps. No one thought it could be done, because the mountains were so steep and snow-covered.

Not only did Hannibal surprise the Roman army by attacking with his army of 40,000 men, but he took along 37 war elephants, too.

The Roman army defeated Hannibal eventually, and after that they made sure no one else could enter their empire. They also began using elephants in war, too.

Materials

Large paper grocery sack

Newspaper

Masking tape

4 short cardboard tubes
(from rolls of toilet paper)

3 cups flour

3 to 5 cups water

Mixing bowl

Spoon

Lightweight cardboard

Scissors

Piece of rope or braided yarn

Tempera or acrylic paints

Paintbrush

Spray paint

Tape a ball of newspapers to the sack for a head.

Tape 4 toilet paper tubes in place for legs.

When the first layers are dry, tape on a newspaper trunk and cardboard ears. Then cover with more strips. Then tape on a tail and paint.

Stuff the sack with crushed newspaper and tape the end closed. Roll and crush newspaper to make a ball for the head. Use tape to attach the head and 4 tubes to the sack to create an elephant shape. Tear the newspaper into strips about 1 inch wide. Mix the flour and water in the mixing bowl, stirring and adding more water until it's like thin pancake batter.

Dip each strip of newspaper into the papier-mâché, pull it through your fingers to take off the excess paste, and press it gently onto the elephant. Cover the whole elephant with one layer of strips, layering the edges of the strips on top of each other.

Cover the elephant with one or two layers. Let it dry overnight. You can use a blow dryer to dry papier-mâché if you want to hurry the project.

When the first layer is dry, cut out ear shapes from lightweight cardboard and twist a piece of newspaper to make a trunk shape. Tape them in place and cover with several layers of pasted strips. Tape on a piece of rope for a tail. When you're satisfied with the elephant, let it dry. Paint it with tempera or acrylic paints. You can follow the same steps to make a baby elephant to march with the parent—just start with a lunch sack instead of a grocery sack.

KEEP A SECRET: CIPHERS

Ancient Greeks used hidden writing, which they called *cryptography*. The Romans copied it from them and added some of their own ideas.

There were a lot of ways to send a secret message. Here's one that was OK if you had plenty of time. A slave's head was shaved, and the message (something short and simple, like "Revolt now!") was tattooed on his scalp. The hair was allowed to grow back, and the slave sent off to his destination. At the other end, the slave had only to say, "Shave my head," and the message would be revealed. It was very clever, especially since the slave couldn't reveal the message he was carrying—he had no way to see it!

Roman general and later emperor Julius Caesar used secret writing all the time. He would sometimes use the third letter after the one he intended. For example, writing *D* to represent *A*, or *E* for *B*. Here's the word *fun* in his cipher: IXQ. To make a key for his type of cipher, just write the alphabet and then put the cipher below it.

regular alphabet
A B C D E F . . .

the cipher
D E F G H I . . .

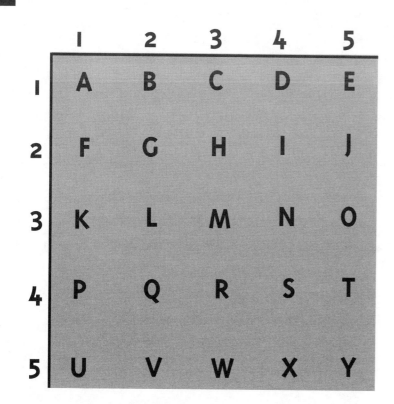

	1	2	3	4	5
1	A	B	C	D	E
2	F	G	H	I	J
3	K	L	M	N	O
4	P	Q	R	S	T
5	U	V	W	X	Y

What's this secret word: 12-15-43?

What would be the use of ciphers without a mail service? The Romans had a system of couriers who carried messages and mail on horseback. They changed horses at stations along the main roads in the empire. These relays of riders could cover more than 144 miles in twenty-four hours. The Pony Express in the western United States was set up the same way.

✴ Make up your own secret writing cipher. To change the cipher, just start with the letter "A" in a different space. Be sure the person you're writing to has a key to the same cipher so he or she can decipher your message.

KEY

Here's a popular Roman cipher called a "blocked alphabet" cipher. By writing the letters of the alphabet in a block, you can come up with a secret cipher. Make a chart numbering 1 through 5 both across and down. Then write the alphabet in the spaces (Z has to be left out). This will be the key to the cipher. To write a message in this secret writing, use the 2 numbers the letter matches. Write the number from the top row first, then the letter from the left row. The letter C is 31. H is 32. Get the idea?

SLAVES

Slave traders followed the armies to get battle captives. Slaves were taken that to the cities and sold in markets. A clay tablet that hung from each slave's neck identified his country, age, and how strong or educated he was. It also told if he had ever committed a crime.

Slaves wore leg irons, chains, or heavy iron collars to keep them from running off. If they tried, they were put in their owner's dungeon prison. Every farm had its own prison. Slaves were beaten and branded on the forehead if they ran away or stole. Some were punished by being hung on a wooden cross or made to fight wild animals in the theater.

In 73 B.C., a gladiator named Spartacus led a slave revolt. He and his followers defeated two Roman armies. The revolt was crushed two years later when six thousand slaves were hung on crosses, or *crucified*, beside the road to Rome for one hundred miles.

COUNTING AND MEASURING

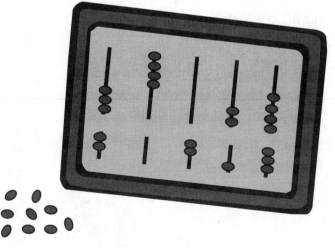

MAKE COINS

At first, people paid for things by bartering or trading what they had for what they wanted. Later, coins were made. During the Roman Empire, most coins had the emperor's head on one side; the other side of the coin had a symbol of his successes. Coins were stamped from gold or silver, but there weren't enough for everyone in the empire. People could pay taxes with farm products or things they made.

Create some coins special to you.

Materials

Synthetic clay, like Sculpey or Fimo

Serrated plastic knife

Toothpick or paper clip

★ Form the clay into a thick log. Use the knife to slice off pieces. Flatten the pieces with your palm and carve designs or words into the clay with the toothpick or paper clip. Bake according to clay package directions with an adult's help or air-dry as directed on the package.

Cut rounds of clay and carve designs into them.

COIN RUBBINGS

You can use the coins you made in the previous activity to do this one.

Materials

Newspaper

Construction paper

Coins

Crayons with paper wrappings removed

Place a thick layer of newspaper on your work surface so making the rubbing will be easier. Place coins under construction paper and, using the side of a crayon, rub color onto the paper. The engraved image of the coin will appear on the paper as you rub.

How much do you know about our coins? Take a look at the penny, sometimes called the Lincoln head penny. The image is of President Abraham Lincoln and was first used on coins to celebrate the one hundredth anniversary of Lincoln's birth, in 1909. It was the first cent to have the motto "In God We Trust" on it. In 1959 the image of the Lincoln Memorial building was put on the back. On the penny, look carefully near Lincoln's chest for the year the coin was made. Below the year is a letter showing where the coin was minted. There are three U.S. mints, in San Francisco, Philadelphia, and Denver. You'll find the letter *S* for San Francisco or *D* for Denver just below the year. If there's no letter, the coin was made in Philadelphia.

Take a look at a nickel. It shows the head of President Thomas Jefferson on one side and his house, called Monticello, on the back. The nickel was designed by Felix Schlag, who won a $1,000 prize in a competition with other artists in 1938.

Today's dime shows the head of President Franklin Roosevelt. A quarter shows the head of President George Washington.

Half dollars made since 1964 show President John Kennedy's head on the front and the coat of arms for the presidency on the back. The coat of arms is an eagle with spread wings holding an olive branch and arrows. There are thirteen arrows, just like the original thirteen colonies. One arrow can be easily broken, but thirteen together can't. The idea came from the Iroquois Confederacy, a partnership of six Native North American nations.

Susan B. Anthony is the only woman ever depicted on an American coin. She worked hard to get the right to vote for American women. She is shown on a dollar coin, made from 1979 to 1981. Looking at the coins you'll notice some words in Latin, the language of the ancient Romans. "E Pluribus Unum" is the motto of the United States. It means "Out of many, one."

ROMAN CALENDAR

In early Roman times there were 355 days and twelve months. Martius (March) was the first month of the year. Julius Caesar changed it to a solar year of 365½ days, based on an earlier Greek calendar. Every fourth year one day was added—the leap year. It was called the Julian Calendar, and the month of March was the beginning of the year until the pope of the Roman Catholic Church changed the first month to January in 1582.

Here are the months, in Caesar's time:

MARTIUS

APRILIS

MAIUS

JUNIUS

QUINCTILIS
(LATER RENAMED JULIUS, AFTER GUESS WHO?)

SEXTILIS
(RENAMED AUGUSTUS, AFTER THE NEXT EMPEROR)

SEPTEMBER

OCTOBER

NOVEMBER

DECEMBER

JANUARIUS

FEBRUARIUS

ROMAN NUMERALS

Ancient Romans didn't have special characters to stand for numbers. They used letters to show numbers. Here are the letters they used and the value of each:

$$I = 1$$
$$V = 5$$
$$X = 10$$
$$L = 50$$
$$C = 100$$
$$D = 500$$
$$M = 1,000$$

To better figure out how to read and write like the Romans did, remember these things:

1. A letter that is repeated, repeat its value that many times.

$$X = 10$$
$$XX = 10 + 10 = 20$$
$$XXX = 10 + 10 + 10 = 30$$
$$C = 100$$
$$CC = 100 + 100 = 200$$

2. Letters placed after another letter of greater value increase the greater number by adding the smaller to it. Add the smaller number to the larger.

$$VI = 5 + 1 = 6$$
$$LXX = 50 + 10 + 10 = 70$$
$$MCC = 1,000 + 100 + 100 = 1,200$$

3. A smaller letter placed before another letter of greater value decreases the greater number by the amount of the smaller number. Subtract the smaller number from the larger.

IX = 1 subtracted from 10 = 9

Here's an easy way to remember Roman numerals: _____ X _____. Smaller amounts on the left side of this equation are subtracted from the larger number to the right. If a smaller number appears on the right side, this is added to the larger number.

I = 1	VI = 6
II = 2	VII = 7
III = 3	VIII = 8
IV = 4	IX = 9
V = 5	X = 10

After the first ten numbers, it gets easier. For the teens, just add numbers after X to show that you've gone higher than 10.

XI = 11
XII = 12
XIII = 13
XIV = 14
XV = 15
XVI = 16
XVII = 17
XVIII = 18
XIX = 19
XX = 20

Counting by tens is even easier:

X = 10
XX = 20
XXX = 30
XL = 40

(Since L = 50, the X in front of the L means subtract 10 from 50, which = 40.)

L = 50
LX = 60
LXX = 70
LXXX = 80
XC = 90

(Since C = 100, the X before the C means subtract 10 from 100, which = 90.)

C = 100

The larger numbers are easy:

D = 500
M = 1,000

Like the Greeks, the Romans didn't have a symbol for zero.

Can you figure out your age? Your grade in school? How about the year? The year 2000? It will be fun to spot the use of Roman numerals today. Look at book chapters, clock faces, and at the end of movies or television programs.

ABACUS

How did Romans multiply with these numerals? They didn't. They used an abacus to do math.

Like all people, the Romans had first used their fingers to count with. The next device they used for counting was a board covered with sand and divided into columns by lines drawn with a finger. Markers were placed along the lines to keep count. The markers were made of clay with a figure of a hand showing different numbers by the position of the fingers.

A more complicated counting device was the *abacus*. At first the abacus was a board with a series of grooves in which pebbles, or *calculi*, were moved as a count was made. That device grew to be the abacus still in use in Asia today. It's made of two rows of wire rods, one row long and one row short. The short rods each hold two beads. The long rods each hold five beads.

Materials

Rectangle of cardboard or Styrofoam tray

Marker

Beans

Markers are dry beans.

In ancient Rome elementary schools taught three things: reading, writing, and arithmetic. Class started at dawn and went without a break until noon. It was held under a tented awning along a street. The teacher had a chair; the students sat on benches. There was a blackboard, some clay tablets, and a few abacuses. Classes were held year-round, except on holidays.

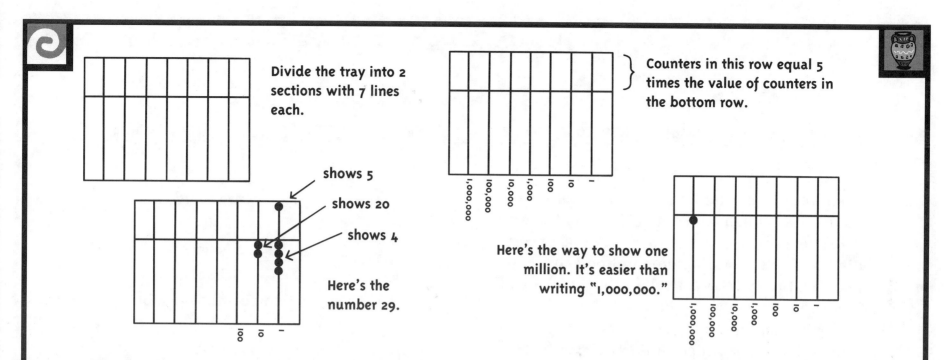

Divide the tray into 2 sections with 7 lines each.

shows 5
shows 20
shows 4

Here's the number 29.

Counters in this row equal 5 times the value of counters in the bottom row.

Here's the way to show one million. It's easier than writing "1,000,000."

⭐ Mark the cardboard with 7 lines running up and down from edge to edge parallel to the shorter sides. Draw another line across, parallel to the longer sides, dividing the tray into two sections, making the bottom section twice as long as the top section.

To count, place beans in position on the lines. The lines begin at the right and move to the left: ones, tens, hundreds, thousands, ten thousands, hundred thousands, and millions. Each line in the top row represents 5 times the value of each line in the bottom row.

That means 1 bean in the ones line of the top row is

equal to 5. One bean in the tens line of the top row is equal to 50. Use the lines in the top row plus the lines in the bottom row to make up a number. One bean in the ones line of the top row plus two beans in the ones line of the bottom equals 7 (5 + 2 = 7). Two beans in the ones line of the top row plus two beans in the ones line of the bottom row is 12 (5 + 5 + 2 = 12).

Once you get the idea, it's fun and easy to do. To show the number 1,000,000 (one million), you just need one bean, in the seventh line of the bottom row—a lot easier than writing all those zeros!

HOW FAR WAS THAT?
MAKE A HODOMETER

It was possible to draw an accurate map of the entire Roman Empire in 20 B.C. because all roads were straight and marked with milestones, placed one thousand paces apart. A huge map was displayed in its own building in Rome. Its most important purpose was to chart the marching of armies.

Romans built their roads straight, going inside tunnels or across bridges if they needed to. The milestones told how far it was to the next city. Sometimes benches were put beside milestones so travelers could rest. Watch for mile markers the next time you travel on a highway. Road engineers today put them up to direct road crews for repairs and to help police and ambulances locate accidents. If your family is stranded and needs to call for help, tell people the number of the nearest mile marker so they can locate you easily. Today, some mile markers tell how far to the county line or state border.

Here's how to make a *hodometer* to measure distance. As the wheel turns around, it measures the same distance every time.

Materials

Cardboard

Ruler

2 Pencils

Scissors

Long cardboard tube
(from a roll of wrapping paper)

Nail

Brass fastener

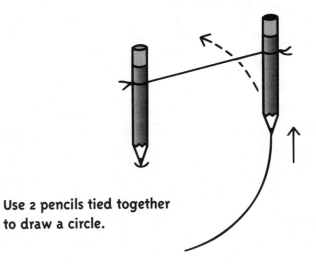

Use 2 pencils tied together to draw a circle.

Fasten the cardboard circle to the long cardboard tube. Roll it on the ground to measure.

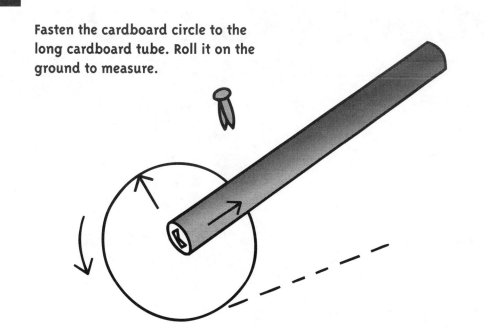

This hodometer will measure a distance of 1 foot, or about 30 centimeters, every time it turns around. You'll need a cardboard circle 10 centimeters across. You can make the correct size circle by making a pencil mark in the center of the cardboard. Use a ruler to measure a distance 5 centimeters away from the penciled mark. Mark it with pencil. Continue measuring and marking all around the center dot, to create the outline of a circle. Use a pencil to connect the marks, and cut out along the penciled line.

Poke a hole in the center of the cardboard with a pencil tip. Poke or punch a hole in the side of the cardboard tube on one end. Use the brass fastener to attach the circle to the tube.

Mark a heavy line on the circle and in a matching spot on the tube. To measure distance, roll the circle along the ground. Every time the two lines meet up, you've gone 1 foot.

HOW DO YOU MEASURE UP?

Romans and many other ancient people used parts of the body to measure distance.

FOOT = length of a foot

DIGIT = width of the index finger

PALM = width of the palm of the hand

CUBIT = the distance from the elbow
to the tip of the longest finger

YARD = arm's length from shoulder
to the tip of the longest finger

FATHOM = the distance between a man's two hands
with his arms spread out

This system was used up to the Middle Ages, but it wasn't a very good way to measure. People are all shapes and sizes, so measurements weren't always exact. See how your own body measures up.

Materials

Lightweight cardboard or construction paper

Pencil

Scissors

Tape measure

Measure and cut a piece of cardboard or construction paper to make your own 1-foot ruler. Step on a piece of paper and mark it around your heel and the tip of your big toe. Do the same for a digit, marking the sides of your index (pointer) finger. Mark your height on a wall and see how many of your feet or digits tall you are.

Use the measuring tape to figure out your own fathom and cubit. Try measuring how many of your cubits wide your room is or how many of your fathoms across your backyard is.

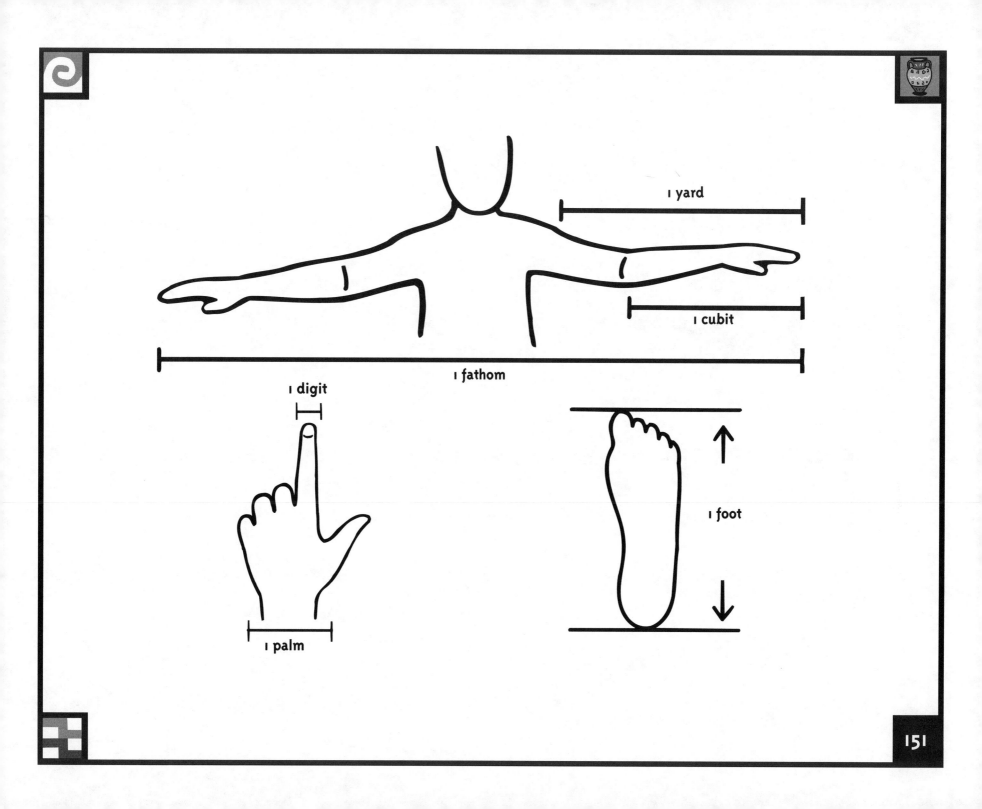

1 yard

1 cubit

1 fathom

1 digit

1 palm

1 foot

HOME SWEET HOME

In the ancient city of Rome there was only one private house for every twenty-six blocks of apartment buildings. Nearly everyone lived in apartments. The buildings were made taller and taller, and they frequently collapsed. A law restricted apartment buildings to sixty-five feet high—about six stories tall. The wealthier people lived on the first floor, or else it was divided into booths and shops. Shopkeepers slept in lofts above the store or workshop. A whole family lived in one room.

Apartments had balconies and open windows (there was no window glass) with pieces of cloth or wooden shutters to keep out rain. People kept potted plants and flowers on the balconies and window ledges.

The walls could be no thicker than a foot and a half (that was a law made to save space in the crowded city). They were built of rows of bricks and stones or pebbles set in concrete. If they didn't collapse, apartment houses often burned down. The wooden floors caught fire from the smoky oil lamps, candles, and torches that people used at night. And there was no water upstairs unless someone carried it up from a street fountain. Not a day passed without several fires in

Rome. Water carriers were slaves who belonged to the owner of a building and were given the duty of carrying vases of water to the building for the residents to use. During the time of the Empire, a group of fire-fighting night watchmen patrolled the streets and reminded people to have pots of water in their apartments.

Rich or poor, Roman homes didn't have much furniture, but for every Roman a bed was the main piece of furniture. People slept on their beds at night but also reclined on them during the day while eating, reading, writing, or visiting with company.

People had the sort of bed they could afford. Some were brick shelves along a wall covered with a pad. Others were big and lavish, carved from wood or made of bronze, silver, and gold. Mattresses were made of cloth and filled with straw, wool, or feathers.

IT'S ALL DOWNHILL—
BUILD AN AQUEDUCT

The city of Rome was built on several hills with the Ebro River flowing through it. The ancient Romans built canals to carry off waste and water. Some canals were built beneath the streets and buildings. Romans even built canals to drain lakes so the land could be farmed. Drinking water was brought to the cities from springs high in the mountains. Sometimes pipes made of lead or baked clay were buried underground to carry the water. Canals were dug in the soil and the sides lined with rocks or bricks. Some are still being used today.

When canals and pipes couldn't be dug, aboveground aqueducts were built. They were made of stone or brick, and the waterway was coated with chalk to keep the water from leaking out. From high in the hills, the aqueducts let water flow right into the city—bringing 300 million gallons of water into Rome every day.

Before the Romans built the aqueducts, they had to work out one problem: People needed to be able to cross to the other side of aqueducts. The aqueducts couldn't be built on top of solid walls. The Romans solved the problem with the *arch*, their favorite building design. By building the wall that held up the aqueduct with arches in it, people, animals, and even rivers could pass beneath the aqueduct while the water ran overhead.

Some arches were over 150 feet high. That's higher than an eight-story building.

Materials

Long cardboard tubes (from rolls of wrapping paper)

Scissors

Aluminum foil

Masking tape

Empty boxes in various sizes, such as a gelatin box, a cake mix box, and a cereal box

Water or marbles

Bowl

In Julius Caesar's time (the beginning of the Roman empire), there were more than one million people living in the city of Rome.

Cut the paper tubes in half the long way. Tape several together. Cover them with aluminum foil to keep the water from soaking through.

Cut arch shapes in the wide sides of the boxes. Stand them up, lined in order from highest to lowest. Tape the aqueduct to the arches. Place the bowl at the end to catch the water or marbles. Pour water or marbles in at the top, and gravity will take the water or marbles to the bottom!

ROMAN MERCHANT SHIP MODEL

Romans needed food and goods brought by ship. The oil, cloth, and wheat that the Romans needed were shipped from other countries because this was the quickest and easiest way to move the large amounts of goods they needed.

Roman merchant ships had two masts and a hold for storing cargo. The ships were wide and sturdily built and could take large loads long distances. Merchant ships were powered by the wind against their cloth sails. Two huge oars at the rear of the ship helped steer it. Besides grain, the ships carried thousands of clay pots, called *amphorae*, filled with wine, oil, and fish sauce. Ships also brought cloth, gems, spices, and thou-

sands of wild animals to Rome for the gladiator fights.

Not all Roman ships carried products. Special warships carried Roman troops in sea battles or to attack distant lands. The troops who went by ship were called *marines*. Warships were powered by hundreds of slave oarsmen who rowed with long wooden oars. There weren't any guns or cannons, because the Romans didn't know about gunpowder. Warships had rams at the front. These were used to knock holes in enemy ships. Marines would also launch flaming balls of fire onto the enemy ships, hoping to start a fire. Wooden ships burned quickly.

Materials

Construction paper

Photocopier or thin paper

Pencil

Scissors

Glue or paste

5 drinking straws

Tape

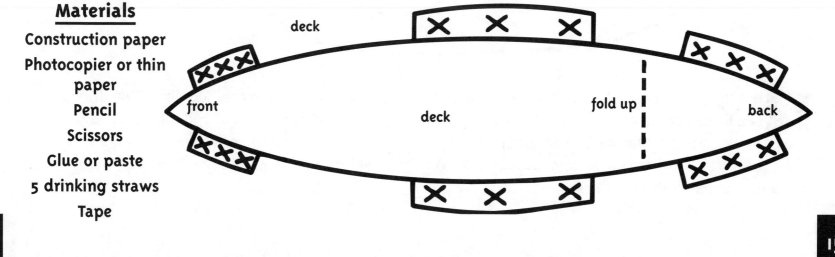

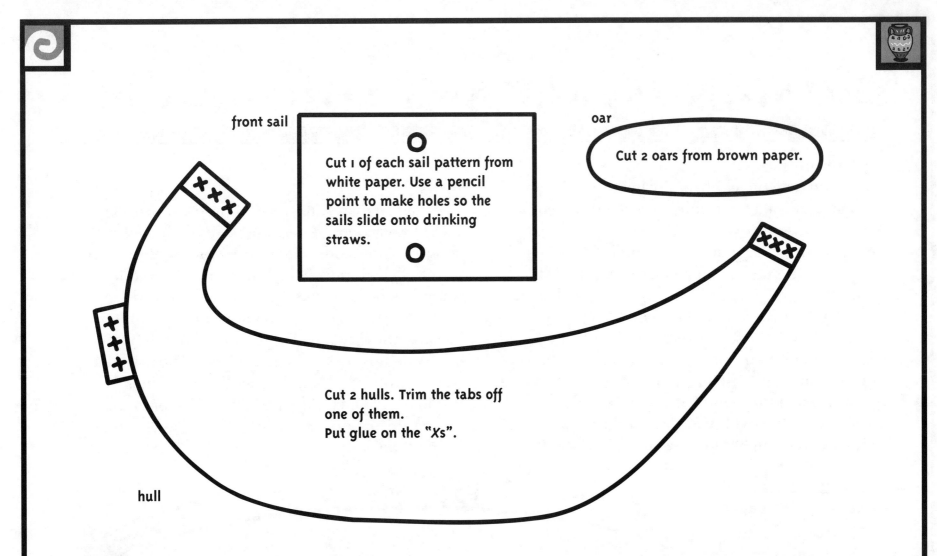

front sail

Cut 1 of each sail pattern from white paper. Use a pencil point to make holes so the sails slide onto drinking straws.

oar

Cut 2 oars from brown paper.

Cut 2 hulls. Trim the tabs off one of them.
Put glue on the "Xs".

hull

Use the pattern to make a paper merchant ship like those used in ancient Rome. Photocopy the page, or trace over the pattern on thin paper. Then cut it out. Use that as a pattern to trace and cut out a fleet of paper ships.

Fold and glue the pieces together. Trim drinking straws to use as masts. Cut and glue each oar to a straw. Tape them in place at the rear of the ship. Cut out white paper sails and glue in place.

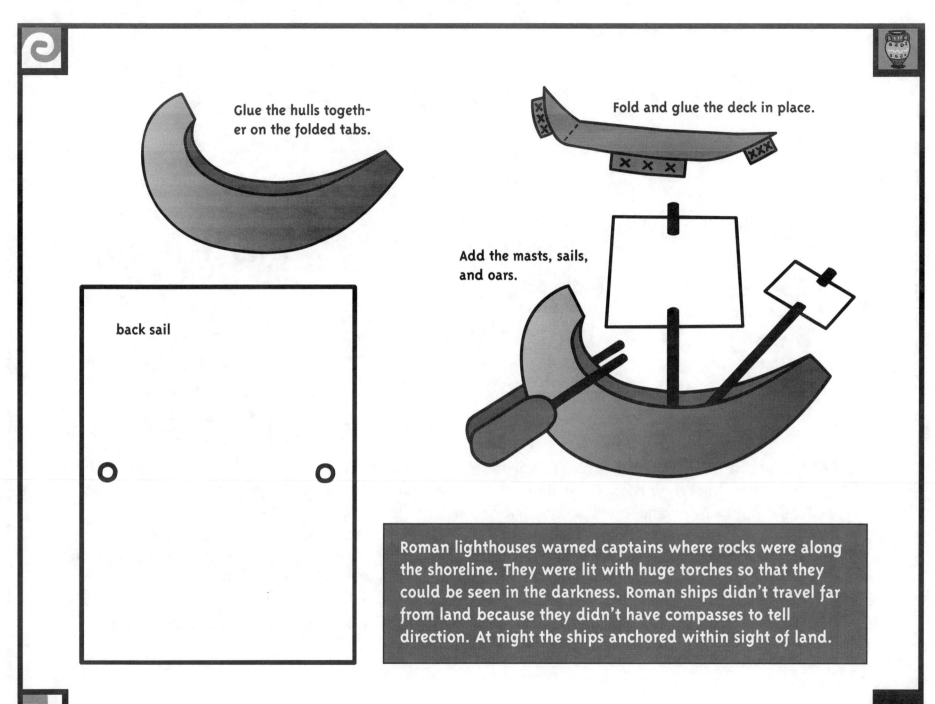

Glue the hulls together on the folded tabs.

Fold and glue the deck in place.

Add the masts, sails, and oars.

back sail

Roman lighthouses warned captains where rocks were along the shoreline. They were lit with huge torches so that they could be seen in the darkness. Roman ships didn't travel far from land because they didn't have compasses to tell direction. At night the ships anchored within sight of land.

WEAVE A MINI BASKET

Romans used baskets for a lot of things. They stored food in baskets at home, took them when shopping at the market, and even used them weighted with stones to anchor boats.

Materials

Paper cup

Pencil

Scissors

Yarn, one color or several

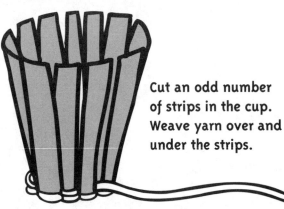

Cut an odd number of strips in the cup. Weave yarn over and under the strips.

⭐ Use the pencil to make marks every ½ inch or about every finger width (your own digit) around the cup. Be sure you have an uneven number of marks. You may have to make one or two marks at less than ½ inch to come out with an uneven number. With scissors, cut from the mark straight to the base of the cup, making an uneven number of strips.

Begin weaving yarn between the strips, starting at the base of the cup. Hide the loose end under the weaving. Weave over and under each strip in a pattern all the way around. After several rows you'll see the way the weaving pattern shows up. Push your weaving down to hide the cup and continue. When you get to the rim, clip the yarn off and tuck the end back under the weaving.

This basket is quick and fun to make, and you can use it as a pencil holder or to display some dried flowers.

WEAVE A MAXIMUS BASKET

This basket is big and can be used as a wastebasket in your bedroom or beside a parent's desk at work.

Materials

Newspaper

Stapler

Pencil

1 9-inch pie plate or dinner plate

2½-inch-thick squares of lightweight cardboard

Lightweight or heavyweight cardboard

Scissors

Spray paint

Daily News Fold in half.

Fold in half again.

Fold in thirds.

Staple to hold.

Make 13.

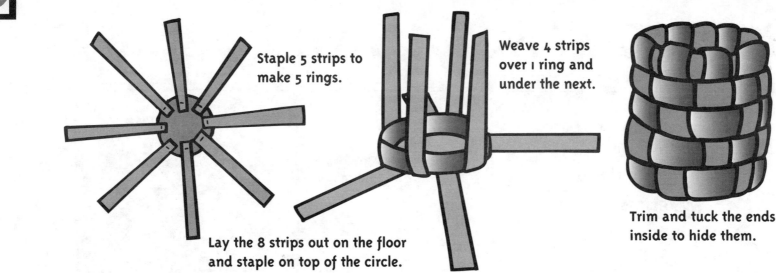

Staple 5 strips to make 5 rings.

Weave 4 strips over 1 ring and under the next.

Lay the 8 strips out on the floor and staple on top of the circle.

Trim and tuck the ends inside to hide them.

Open a single sheet of newspaper so that it is placed in front of you as if you were going to read it. Begin to fold the newspaper from the bottom. Fold it in half and then in half again. Then fold it in thirds. Crease firmly and staple it in 2 or 3 places to hold the folds. Lay this aside and make 12 more folded strips exactly like the first one. (This will give you thirteen strips—an uneven number, needed for weaving.)

Trace around the pie pan on a piece of cardboard to make 1 9-inch circle. Then make a second circle on another piece of cardboard. Cut them out. Lay 1 circle on the floor and place 8 of the newspaper strips, arranged to extend like spokes of a wheel, across the plate. Staple the ends of the newspaper

strips to the circle. Take the 5 remaining newspaper strips and staple the ends together to form 5 individual rings.

Lift every other strip upright (for a total of 4). Slip 1 of the newspaper circles down over them. Release these 4 strips and lift the remaining 4 up. Slip a newspaper ring over them. Continue in this manner, weaving the newspaper strips until you have used all 5 rings. Trim and tuck the ends of the newspaper strips under the top ring on the inside or outside.

Glue the remaining cardboard circle to the bottom of the basket to cover the rough ends. Go outside and spray-paint your basket. Work on old newspapers, spraying a couple of light coats to avoid drips.

WREATHS OR CROWNS?

During the Roman Republic, elected officials and con-suls wore crowns made of leaves. Julius Caesar, the first dictator to declare himself emperor, wore a crown of gold leaves, and the emperors after him did, too. When Nero became emperor he had a crown made of gold with points to look like the rays of the sun.

Materials

#20 wire

Wire cutter

Green floral tape (available at craft stores)

Silk flowers and leaves

Glue gun

Gold spray paint (if desired)

✶ Wrap a piece of wire around your head, and then snip the end off about 4 inches longer. Wrap the ends of the wire around each other to make the wreath frame.

Wrap floral tape around the wire until it's completely covered. Use a glue gun to stick flowers and leaves all over the wreath frame. Use pieces of floral tape to cover any ends or stems that stick out.

Wear your crown to a banquet, parade, or festival just like patricians did.

If you feel more like an emperor or empress, spray the crown with gold spray paint. Work outdoors on old newspapers, spraying a couple of light coats to avoid drips.

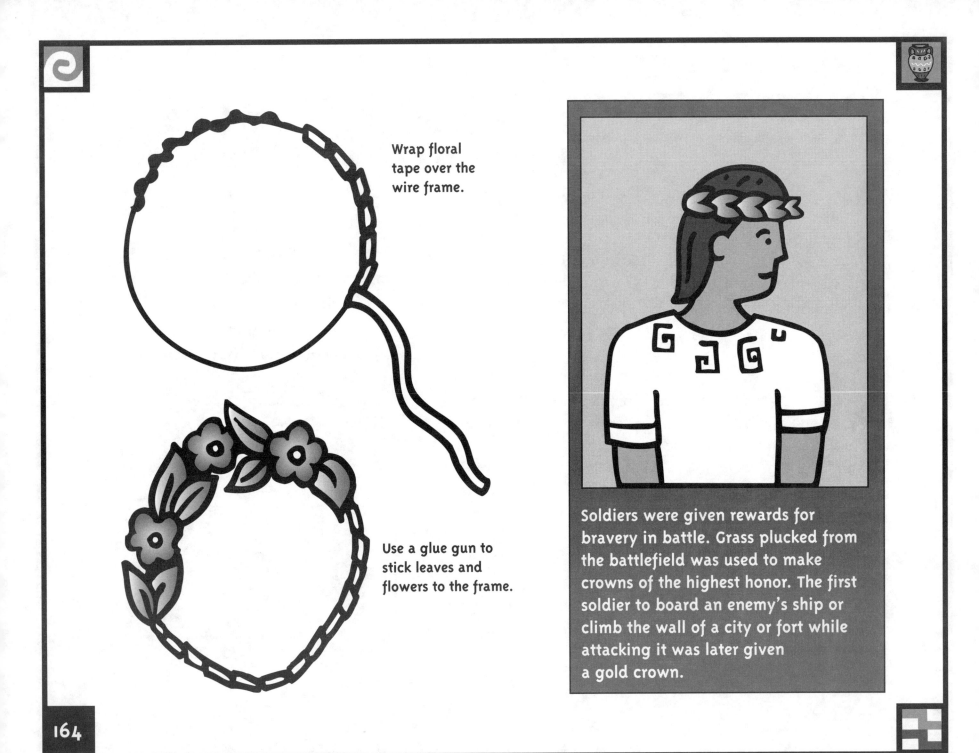

Wrap floral tape over the wire frame.

Use a glue gun to stick leaves and flowers to the frame.

Soldiers were given rewards for bravery in battle. Grass plucked from the battlefield was used to make crowns of the highest honor. The first soldier to board an enemy's ship or climb the wall of a city or fort while attacking it was later given a gold crown.

WAX TABLETS

In about 50 B.C. thin sheets of wood were first tied together with leather laces to make a book. A layer of wax covered each wooden page. To write on the page, a person scratched the wax with a pointed tool called a *stylus*. It had a smooth end with which to rub out mistakes.

Romans used these wax tablets for all kinds of simple letters, lists, or notes. Archaeologists found an old tablet that was a shopping list taken to the market.

Roman schoolboys were taught to read and write by tracing their finger over a letter and then copying it on wax tablets. Some used wooden boards with letters cut into the surface. A boy traced his pen in the grooves to practice writing the letters. Alphabet letters were carved in ivory from elephant tusks and given to children as toys to help them learn the alphabet, sort of like the little plastic letters today.

CRAYON ENGRAVING

★ Put several layers of newspaper on the tabletop as padding beneath the construction paper. It makes coloring with crayons easier and smoother.

Use several bright colors (except black) to color the entire surface of the paper. Press firmly as you color so the colors are bright.

Mix liquid dish soap into black tempera paint. (The soap will help the paint stick to the slick waxy surface of the crayon.) Paint over the entire surface of the crayoned paper with the mixture. Let it dry.

When the black paint is dry it's time to do the engraving. Put a fresh layer of newspaper under your work again, both as a pad and because this part is messy.

Use the tip of a nail or an opened paper clip to make a drawing or design by gently scratching through the paint layer. The scratching reveals the bright crayon color glowing through. Don't like the design? Repaint with tempera, let it dry, and engrave again!

Materials

Newspaper

Construction paper

Crayons

1 tablespoon liquid dish soap

1 pint black tempera paint

Paintbrush

Nail or opened paper clip

Educated slaves had to read aloud to their masters during mealtime or in the baths. They had to write their letters, copy books for the library, and take care of the family's book collection.

Paint over the crayoned surface.

Scratch out a design or image. The crayon colors will show up when the paint is scratched away.

The children of ancient Rome learned to write using stylus pens on wax tablets. Romans also wrote on papyrus sheets using reeds or metal pens and ink made from soot.

GAMES

The Romans had a lot of ways to enjoy their free time. They could attend the theater, watch chariot races, or see gladiators combat each other or wild animals. They went to the baths every day, where people also played ball games, board games, and dice games. Children's toys were dolls, toy soldiers, and animals. Walnuts were used like marbles, and hoops were rolled along the ground with sticks.

MICATIO

M icatio is a game for two players that can be played anywhere, anytime. The two players each raise the fingers of their right hands at the same time, keeping the rest of their fingers folded down. They change the number of fingers they raise each time they do this. As they raise fingers at the same time, they each call out the number they guess to be the total number of fingers raised by both. They keep playing until one player guesses correctly and wins.

In Micatio players must call out their guesses as they show their hands to each other.

ODD OR EVEN

Even the emperor's family played this game. In odd or even, the players guess whether the number of pebbles or nuts hidden in the other player's hand is an odd or even number.

JACKS

Toss the 5 bones into the playing area with one hand. To play, toss the ball up into the air while you scoop up the bones with one hand and catch the ball before it hits the ground. Start with 1 bone, scooping it up with one hand and catching the ball in the same hand. Drop that bone back on the playing area. Toss the ball again, and scoop up 2 bones and then the ball. Continue until you can scoop up all 5 bones and the ball in one turn. If you miss—not scooping the right number of bones or missing the ball—it's the next player's turn.

Materials
5 small bones, from chicken wings, or steak, or oxtail

Small ball

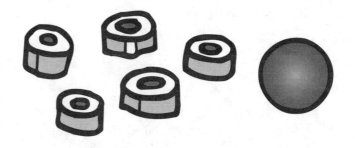

DICE

It was against the law to gamble money on dice games in ancient Rome, but this didn't keep people from enjoying this game.

★ (Adult help suggested.)
Roll the clay out flat to about ½ inch thick. Cut it into squares. These will be your dice. Mark the dice with the end of a drinking straw and a pencil point, so they look like they came from ancient Rome. Roman dice weren't exact cubes; they weren't the same size all around. They were more like square tiles.

Bake the dice as directed on the clay package.

To play, take turns tossing the dice and adding up the scores. Whoever has the highest number of points wins. You can make up your own rules.

Materials
Rolling pin or dowel
Synthetic clay, like Sculpey or Fimo
Serrated plastic knife
Drinking straw
Pencil

Use a drinking straw and a pencil to mark the dice.

TRIGON

Trigon is a ball game the ancient Romans played at the baths. Three players stand in corners of a large triangular area. They throw balls to each other without warning, tossing with one hand and catching balls thrown at them with the other. The goal is not to drop a ball. They didn't have rubber balls. Balls were actually sewn pieces of animal skin filled with sand, feathers, dirt, flour, or round beanbags.

173

MAKING LATIN SMALL TALK

Greeks spoke what we call old Greek, and Romans spoke Latin. Many languages spoken today are based on Latin, like Romanian, Portuguese, French, Spanish, and Italian. No living people now speak in Latin except people who study it. It's called a *dead language.* Try saying some words the way the ancient Romans did:

Latin	English
Salve	Hello
Vale	Good-bye
Gratias	Thank you
Gratias maximus	Thank you very much
Faustum diem	Good morning
Felicem noctem	Good night
Hora est	What time is it?
Te deinceps videbo	See you later

CAVE CANEM

Here are some long-popular Latin sayings that people use today:

Latin	English
Carpe diem	Seize the day" or "Do it now"
Caveat emptor	"Buyer beware" or "Buy at your own risk"
Cave canem	"Beware of the dog"

GIVE A READING

Emperor Caesar opened a state library in Rome, copying the Greek one at Alexandria. The provinces soon built libraries, too. Bookstores opened where scrolls were copied and sold. Bookstores had walls covered with cubbies to hold scrolls. Teams of slaves were making copies all day long. The booksellers didn't pay writers; they just copied the books. Writers tried to get attention and some money by holding public readings. They would read their work as they finished each chapter. Even emperors read their poetry to audiences. Wealthy Romans set aside rooms in their houses that they called *auditoriums* just for writers to read their work to guests. There was a small stage at one end of the room where the reader sat. A curtain hung in front of her where people could listen without the readers being seen. In front of the reader, the audience sat on benches. They were invited by notes delivered to their homes. Writers depended on wealthy people letting them read in their auditoriums. Practical people rented out their auditoriums for cash.

Writers weren't a bit shy. They unrolled their scrolls wherever people were: in the market, at the forum, in the baths. Some even stood on street corners and read out loud to passersby. Romans were reading their poems, stories, speeches, and plays out loud all the time—morning and evening, winter and summer.

If you've never read your own writing to someone, give it a try. If you're shy, try reading something written by someone else first and then read your own creation. Practice reading aloud ahead of time. Be sure to speak slowly and clearly and pick something that will interest the listener. Smile before you start, and remember that, like everything, practice makes perfect!

VOLCANO ALERT!

In A.D. 79 Mount Vesuvius, a sleeping volcano, erupted. It hurled volcanic ash, lava, and stone in the air and buried the towns of Pompeii and Herculaneum. The mud over Herculaneum was sixty-six feet deep. Everything and everyone who didn't run was buried deep beneath the ash and lava. In Pompeii, there was no mud, only a light fall of ash, like powdery dust, at first. But it quickly turned to larger pellets and globs of pumice rocks each weighing many pounds. Clouds of sulfur fumes settled on the town. People who hid from the pelting rocks were smothered by the fumes. Two days later when the sun came out, both towns were destroyed. The land was ruined for eleven miles around, and ash blew all the way to Africa. The buried towns were never rebuilt.

Seventeen hundred years later, archaeologists discovered the towns, began digging into the layers of earth, and learned about what life in Pompeii had been like. They found where bodies had been covered with ash or mud right where they were when the volcano blew. The archaeologists didn't find the actual bodies of the ancient Pompeians, because they had disintegrated long ago. The bodies had left holes in the ash. Scientists poured plaster into the holes, using the hardened ash as a mold. The plaster casts preserved the impressions where the bodies had been and even details like clothing and sandals appeared. They made casts of a chained pet dog and some of looters who were caught in the gas because they had stayed behind to steal.

BUILD A VOLCANO

Materials

Newspaper

Paper cup

½ cup baking soda

Coffee mug

Bowl

Construction paper

Scissors

Tape

Food coloring

1 cup vinegar

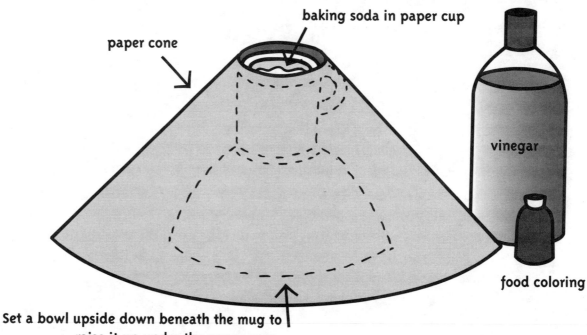

paper cone

baking soda in paper cup

vinegar

food coloring

Set a bowl upside down beneath the mug to raise it up under the paper cone.

⭐ Cover the work area with several layers of news-paper or work outdoors—this gets messy!

Put baking soda in the paper cup. Slip the cup inside the coffee mug to keep it from tipping over. Set the mug on top of an upside-down bowl. Shape a cone from a large half circle of construction paper. Trim it to fit around the mug and bowl to look like a mountain. Tape it in place.

Squirt a few drops of several different food colors into the baking soda.

Slowly pour vinegar into the baking soda, and the volcano will erupt—you'll have flowing colored foam as long as you keep adding vinegar!

THE END

The Roman Empire became so huge that it was divided into two sections, the east and the west. Two capitals were set up to govern, the city of Rome in the western half and the city of Constantinople in the eastern half. But the cost of maintaining two capitals and large armies and governing so large an empire made taxes very high. Invaders attacked parts of the spread-out empire and, in 410 B.C., the Visigoths invaded the city of Rome. Forty-five years later the Vandals from Scandinavia invaded. These wars may have weakened the Roman Empire.

We don't really know why the Romans didn't fight back when the invaders came. Some people today think it was because the invaders brought diseases like malaria to Rome that the people had no immunity against; thus they were too sick to fight. Other people think the lead pipes and cooking pots the Romans used had poisoned their bodies with lead. Some point out that the people of the Roman Empire were too restricted by government and that they didn't care if the empire came to a close. During this time many Romans moved to the countryside to escape the troubles of living in the city and having a restrictive government.

Some people think this is what caused the city's collapse. Many new people streamed into the Roman Empire from Europe and Asia, and the well-organized system that had been the great Roman Empire gave way to a variety of new countries and smaller kingdoms. Scholars are still trying to discover the reasons why the Roman Empire fell.

The old city of Rome still exists, now as the capital of Italy. Many ruins left by the Romans are scattered throughout Europe. You can still see bits of old roads, aqueducts, coliseums, and other buildings erected by the Romans. Because they were well designed and made of stone, they have lasted for centuries.

BIBLIOGRAPHY

Africa, Thomas W. *The Ancient World*. Boston: Houghton Mifflin Company, 1969

American Heritage Dictionary of the English Language, Third ed. Boston: Houghton Mifflin, 1992.

Aristotle. *Constitution of Athens and Related Texts*. Kurt Von Fritz and Ernst Kapp, eds. New York: Hafner Publishing Company, 1950.

Barber, Elizabeth Wayland. *Women's Work: The First 20,000 Years*. New York: W. W. Norton & Company, 1994.

Billstein, Rick, and Shlomo Libeskind and Johnny W. Lott. *A Problem Solving Approach to Mathematics for Elementary Teachers, Second ed*. Menlo Park, CA: The Benjamin Cummings Publishing Company, 1984.

Boren, Henry C. *The Ancient World: An Historical Perspective*. Englewood Cliffs, NJ: Prentice-Hall, Inc., 1976.

Carcopino, Jerome. *Daily Life in Ancient Rome*. London: Penguin Books, 1941, 1970.

Ceram, C. W. *Gods, Graves, and Scholars: The Story of Archaeology*. New York: Alfred A. Knopf, 1967.

Hamilton, Edith. *The Roman Way*. New York: W. W. Norton & Co., 1932.

Heddens, James W. and William R. Speer. *Today's Mathematics*, Sixth ed. Chicago: Science Research Associates, 1988.

Kohler, Carl. *A History of Costume*. New York: Dover Publications, Inc., 1963.

Leon, Vicki. *Uppity Women of Ancient Times*. Berkeley, CA: Conari Press, 1995.

Logan, Robert. *The Alphabet Effect*. New York: William Morrow & Company, 1986.

McKeever, Susan. *Ancient Rome*. New York: Dorling Kindersley Publishing, 1995.

Quest for the Past. *Reader's Digest*. Pleasantville, NY: Reader's Digest Associates, Inc., 1984.

Rothschild, Henry R. *Biocultural Aspects of Disease*. New York: Academic Press, 1981.

Schnurnberger, Lynn. *Let There Be Clothes: 40,000 Years of Fashion*. New York: Workman Publishing, 1991.

700 Science Experiments for Everyone. UNESCO. New York: Doubleday and Co., 1958.

Singer, Charles. *A Short History of Scientific Ideas to 1900*. London: Oxford University Press, 1960.

Smith, Jeff. *The Frugal Gourmet Cooks Three Ancient Cuisines: China, Greece, and Rome*. New York: William Morrow and Co., 1990.

Smith, Laurence Dwight. *Cryptography: The Science of Secret Writing*. New York: W. W. Norton, 1943.

Sokolov, Raymond. *Why We Eat What We Eat*. New York: Summit Books, 1991.

Veyne, Paul, ed. *A History of Private Life: From Pagan Rome to Byzantium*. Cambridge: Harvard University Press, 1987.

Visser, Margaret. *The Rituals of Dinner*. New York: Grove Weidenfeld, 1991.

Yeoman, R. S. *A Guide Book of United States Coins*. Racine, WI: Western Publishing Co., 1983.

INDEX

MORE BOOKS BY **LAURIE CARLSON** FROM **CHICAGO REVIEW PRESS**

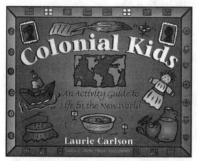

COLONIAL KIDS
An Activity Guide to Life in the New World

Young adventurers can learn about the settling of America while enjoying activities like stitching a sampler, pitching horseshoes, making an almanac, churning butter, and more.

"Colonial America comes to life in this attractive and easy-to-use book."
—*School Library Journal*

". . . the projects offer insight into the colonists' daily life."
—*Publishers Weekly*

ages 5–12   ISBN 1-55652-322-X
160 pages, paper, $12.95

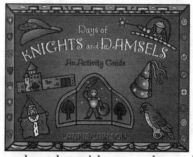

DAYS OF KNIGHTS AND DAMSELS
An Activity Guide

". . . a project-stuffed activity guide to the Middle Ages."
—*Home Education Magazine*

"This book helps you experience the era of kings, queens, and castles with more than a hundred easy projects straight out of the Middle Ages."
—*FACES*

ages 5–12   ISBN 1-55652-291-6
184 pages, paper, $14.95

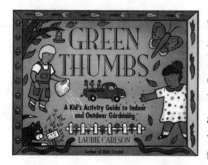

GREEN THUMBS
A Kid's Activity Guide to Indoor and Outdoor Gardening

With a few seeds, some water and soil, and this book, kids will be creating gardens of their own in no time.

"Carlson is an expert at suggesting imaginative activities. Fun, as well as educational."
—*Skipping Stones*

ages 5–12   ISBN 1-55652-238-X
144 pages, paper, $12.95

KIDS CAMP!
Activities for the Backyard or Wilderness

Laurie Carlson and Judith Dammel

Young campers will build an awareness of the environment, learn about insect and animal behavior, boost their self-esteem, and acquire all the basic skills for fun, successful camping.

"A good guide to outdoor adventures for inexperienced young campers and their families."   —*School Library Journal*

ages 5–12   ISBN 1-55652-237-1
184 pages, paper, $12.95

MORE THAN MOCCASINS

A Kid's Activity Guide to Traditional North American Indian Life

Kids will discover traditions and skills handed down from the people who first settled this continent.

"As an educator who works with Indian children I highly recommend [More Than Moccasins] for all kids and teachers. . . . I learned things about our Indian world I did not know."

— Bonnie Jo Hunt
Wicahpi Win (Star Woman)
Standing Rock Lakota

ages 5–12   ISBN 1-55652-213-4
200 pages, paper, $12.95

WESTWARD HO!

An Activity Guide to the Wild West

Cowboys and cowgirls explore the West with activities such as sewing a sunbonnet, panning for gold, cooking flapjacks, singing cowboy songs, and much more.

"Crafts, recipes, songs, and games teamed with an engaging text will have young readers convinced that they're just having fun. . . . Will be heavily used by teachers in the classroom and by children at home."

— *School Library Journal*

"Informative, well-designed, and expertly written."

— *Children's Bookwatch*

ages 5–12   ISBN 1-55652-271-1
160 pages, paper, $12.95